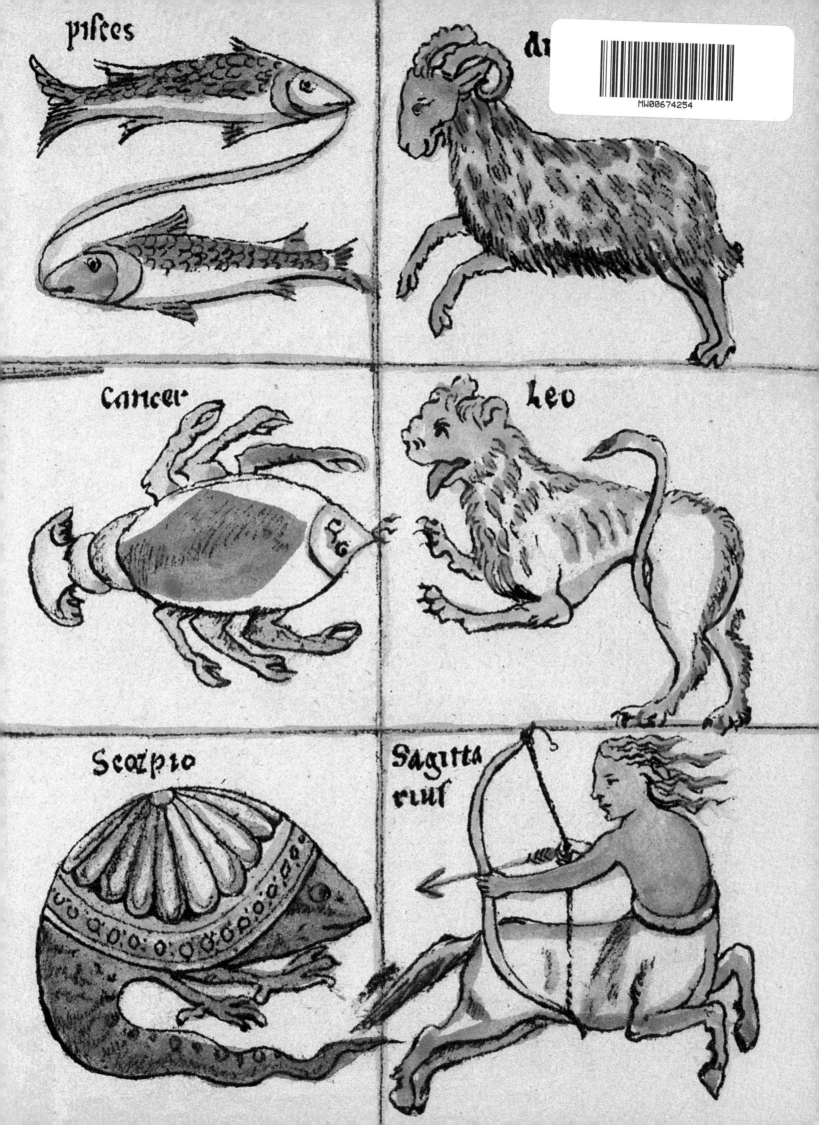

SYMBOLS OF
ASTROLOGY

First published in the United States of America by
Assouline Publishing
601 West 26th Street, New York, NY 10001
www.assouline.com

Copyright for the text © 2000 Editions Assouline, Paris
English translation © 2000 Editions Assouline, Paris

Distributed to the U.S. trade by St. Martin's Press, New York
and in Canada by McClelland & Stewart

ISBN: 2 84323 185 X

Translated by Chanterelle Translations, London
Copy-editing by Christina Henry de Tessan

Color separation: Gravor, Switzerland
Printed and bound by G. Canale & C. S.p.A., Italy

Front cover: Aquarius. French illuminated manuscript, 15th century.
Back cover: illumination from an astrology manuscript. Bohemia, 15th century.
Pages 6–7 : Map of the sky. Detail of a fresco on the ceiling of the
Villa Farnese. Italy, late 16th century.

SYMBOLS OF ASTROLOGY

MICHAËL DELMAR

ASSOULINE

To Jacqueline and Raymond, my parents.
To Louise, Laure, Laurence, Alexis, Phénix,
Marlon, Joïa, Lara, So Kheng, and Gaïa,
children of the Age of Aquarius.

CONTENTS

INTRODUCTION

ASTROLOGY IS A WONDERFUL WAY TO DIS-
COVER THE HUMAN SOUL. IT OFFERS THOSE
WHO TAKE THE TROUBLE TO STUDY ITS SYM-
bols the keys to understanding the universe,
beyond appearances and the physical laws; it
touches upon the mystery of existence. What
other discipline, with the exception of meta-
physics, so integrates the sky and the Earth,
human beings and their environment, yesterday
and today? Astrology is not a religion, but it
forms a bond between human beings—at least
those who have looked to the Heavens to try
and find a sign there.

It is no accident that signs are mentioned frequently in astrology. Human beings, lost in the
cosmos, seek landmarks, and astrology supplies
many of these. There are the temporal landmarks, the seasons, inspired by the cycles of the
sun and the moon; psychological landmarks, the
signs of the zodiac; and even predictions of better times when the conjunctions will be more
favorable and life happier. Astrology today
speaks of a future of brotherly love heralded by
the Age of Aquarius, in which the spiritual
being will know how to exchange and share with
others as he explores the cosmos. As we approach this new age with trepidation, astrology
is assuming greater importance. It represents a
tool for self-knowledge and knowledge of others,
a link between human beings and a bridge to
other cultures.

Since astrology acknowledges the important
role played by intuition, it is considered one of
the divinatory arts, rather than a science. But
science, as it is practiced in the West, is only one
room in the house of God. Astrology is the win-
dow, opening on the universe and contemplat-
ing eternity. That is why, as Albert Einstein
wrote (*Cosmic Religion,* 1934), "it is a sort of
elixir for humanity."

Astronomer Observing the Sky, *Johannes Hevelius. Print, 1647.*

THE FIRST OBSERVATORIES

STANDING STONES AND ZIGGURATS

"That which is below is like that which is above."

HERMES TRISMEGISTUS (*The Emerald Table*, 4th century)

THE DIALOGUE BETWEEN MAN AND THE SKY HAS HAD RELIGIOUS CONNOTATIONS SINCE THE DAWN OF HISTORY. ONE OF THE FIRST astronomical observatories, the Tower of Jericho, was built some seven thousand years B.C. It was thirty feet high and consisted of a flight of twenty-eight steps cut into blocks of stone, as many steps as there were days in the lunar cycle. This tower, which was the precursor of the Mesopotamian ziggurats, was also a place of worship. The moon thus reigned over the Other Side, death and resurrection.

The ruins left behind by ancient civilizations all over the world contain evidence of an established fascination for the cosmos, and provide proof that the celestial mechanisms were understood in some depth. Some archaeological sites show alignments designed to relate to certain celestial phenomena such as solstices or eclipses. The builders of these monuments worshiped the sun and the moon, performed sacrifices and practiced a religion which worshiped the dead. Archaeological and astronomical research has established a link between the cycles of the cosmos and the celebration of religious festivals. Many sacred alignments, however, continue to be a mystery. The megalithic site of Carnac, near the

Bay of Quiberon, in Brittany, France, which has many such alignments, may date from between 6700 and 4700 B.C. Around the edge of this observatory, researchers have discovered eight lines all converging on the Great Menhir of Locmariaquer, the largest standing stone in Europe. These lines relate to the most significant risings of the moon, especially those which correspond to its fullest and smallest phases.

The shrine at Godmanchester, England, built around 3000 B.C., makes it possible to identify solstices and equinoxes. The architect priests were thus able to guarantee the continuity of the cycle of the seasons, whose importance for agriculture was vital.

Stonehenge, which was created in about 3000 B.C. and rebuilt in around 2100 B.C., operated like a circular slide-rule, providing proof of the accuracy of the prediction of eclipses. The ring of stone lintels, the most remarkable feature of the site, formed lines of sight directed at the main points at which the moon and the sun rise. The Stonehenge alignments intersect almost at right angles to the astral bodies. Gerald Hawkins, an American astronomer, has shown how the computer can be used to understand what techniques were used to make the relevant calculations during the Stone Age! (*Stonehenge Decoded*, 1965.) The special features of the site are directly linked to its latitude, which also happens to be

Rows of standing stones at Carnac. 6700–4700 B.C.

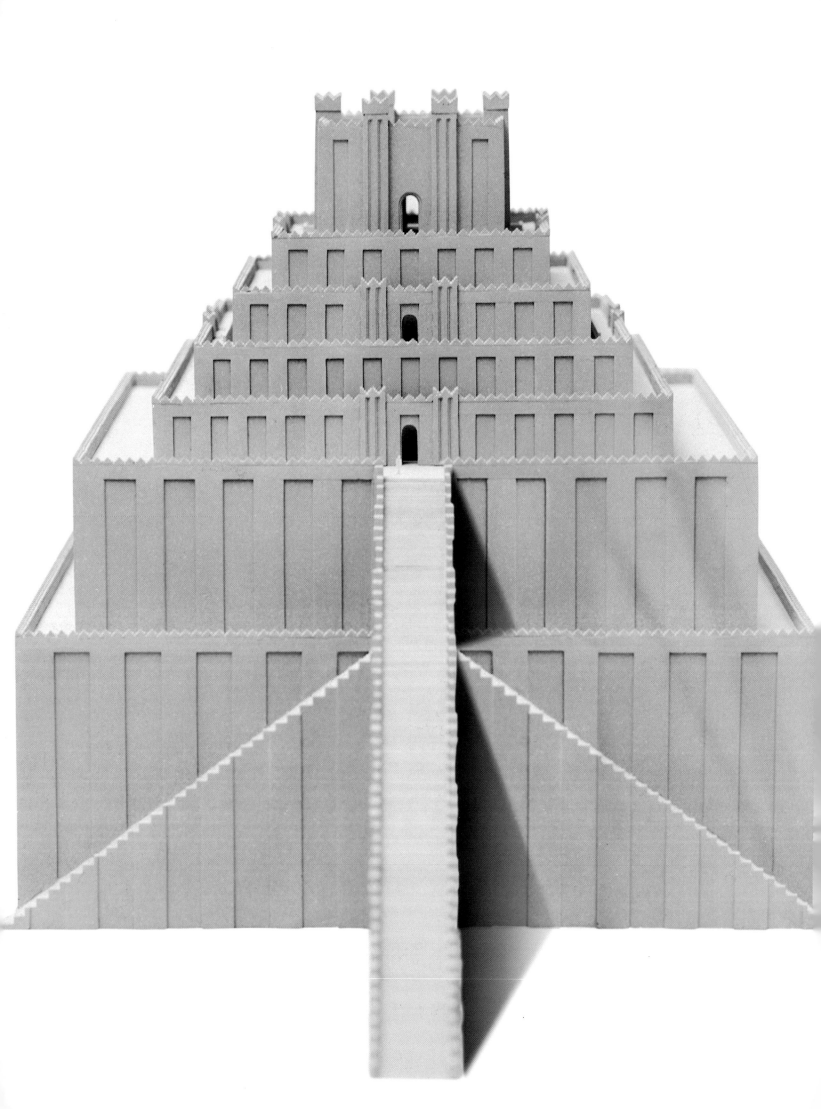

that of the Great Pyramid of Giza, in Egypt, built circa 2600 B.C. These ancient civilizations combined religion and astronomy, and considered the cycle of the seasons parallel to the cycle of life, death and resurrection. One can only marvel at the ability of the ancients to establish such precise astronomical measurements and reproduce them at ground level.

From the earliest speculations right up to modern times, astronomy, an objective science, has been closely linked to astrology, which seeks the transcendental meaning of existence. In the beginning, however, astrology contained a marked tendency to fatalism. The skies belonged to the gods, the Earth to man, who had to obey their laws. The stars and planets made it possible to foretell and interpret the divine will.

The Chaldeans—one of the ancient Semitic peoples of Babylonia—were the founders of astral divination. Archaeological digs at Nineveh and Babylon have uncovered tablets written in cuneiform writing, which are covered with observations of the heavens. The polytheistic religion of the Babylonians was closely linked to predictions, and featured other forms of divination, as through the smoke of incense and the study of the entrails of animal sacrifices. The Chaldeans recognized the sun as the centre of the universe, and were also the first to understand the lunar influence on the tides, and observe the passage of Halley's comet. As for the study of the constella-

tions, this dates back to the reign of Hammurabi, circa 1730 B.C. In order to study the Heavens, the astrologer-priests who were responsible for interpreting the message of the planets, used ziggurats, structures in the shape of a tower or pyramid. The ziggurat at Ur, in present-day Iraq, was built circa 2050 B.C., and is partially preserved. The ziggurat of Babylon (circa 600 B.C.), but now destroyed, consisted of a series of superimposed terraces. It was considered to be one of the Seven Wonders of the Ancient World and may well be the model for the biblical story of the Tower of Babel. It was the Chaldeans in the seventh century B.C. who discovered the planets Jupiter, Mercury, Mars and Venus. But it was not until the fourth century B.C. that the twelve signs of the zodiac were finally codified.

Astrology developed on the basis of Babylonian and Persian beliefs, embracing elements of Egyptian cosmology and Greek philosophy. In its classic form, including its zodiacal theories, it was developed mainly during the Hellenistic Period (after 334 B.C.). This was the age in which Greek civilization spread throughout the known world and heavily influenced various cultures, from the Mediterranean to northern India, in the wake of the conquests of Alexander the Great. "God distributed the stars throughout the vault of the Heavens, so that it became a real cosmos, adorned throughout with their embroidery." (Plato, *Timaeus*, 367 B.C.).

The ziggurat of Babylon (plaster model), built circa 605–562 B.C.

MAP OF THE SKY

INFLUENCES OF BIRTH

THE CASTING OF PERSONAL HOROSCOPES DATES BACK TO THE MOST ANCIENT TIMES. ONCE THE EXCLUSIVE PREROGATIVE OF royalty, the nobility, and dignitaries, the art has been democratized in the computer age. To create a map of the Heavens, it is necessary to know the subject's date, month, year, and precise time of birth. You need an atlas, information about the world's time zones, an ephemeris and a table of the Houses, paper and drawing pencils . . .

CELESTIAL SPHERE,
TERRESTRIAL SPHERE, LOCAL SPHERE

Creating an astral chart is a tricky operation which requires certain mathematical skills. All the stars are distributed throughout a sphere of an indeterminate radius, whose center is the place of birth. This *celestial sphere* extends and enlarges the *terrestrial sphere*, divided into two hemispheres by the equator. Astrology is based on a geocentric, and even anthropocentric, representation of the cosmos. It therefore seeks to establish the position of the planets in relation to the terrestrial coordinates of human beings in their birth setting. That is how the astrologers invented *domification*, or the division of the *local sphere* into twelve Houses to each of which tradition has given a special meaning.

The map of the sky is oriented along two axes. The horizon defines the *Ascendant;* the sign which rises in the east of the chart is called the *ascendant sign*. It colors and affects the characteristics of the

sun sign but is not more important than that sign and does not gain in importance with time, as is sometimes claimed. The meridian of the place of birth determines the position of the *Mid-Sky*. At the opposite of these two points there are the *Descendant* and the *Bottom-of the-Sky*. These four points, or *cuspids*, define the angular Houses which are considered important.

TIME PROBLEMS

Solving the problem of how to measure time universally has long preoccupied amateur astrologers. With the advent of astrology software, this difficulty has largely been removed. In fact, the position of the planets and domification obey two very distinct measurements of time. The positions of the planets published in the ephemeris are measured on the basis of Greenwich Mean Time, the prime Meridian by international agreement. It is expressed in terms of *Universal Time* (UT). Domification, however, is based on *Sidereal Time* (ST) and is different depending on whether the birth takes place in the Northern or the Southern Hemisphere. Account must also be taken of time zones: summer time and double summer time, occupied zones, protectorates, etc. Solving these problems is a delicate matter and involves a certain number of calculations using logarithmic tables. Thus, it is much easier to leave all that to a computer and concentrate on the most interesting aspect of astrology, namely, the interpretation of the map of the sky.

Facing: illumination from an astrology manuscript. Bohemia, 14th century.
Following pages: map of the heavens. Late 18th century.

THE FOUR ELEMENTS

EXPERIMENTATION AND ALCHEMY

MAN DISPLAYED A NEED TO UNDERSTAND THE NATURE OF THINGS AT A VERY EARLY STAGE IN HIS DEVELOPMENT. PRIMITIVE KNOWLEDGE of the elements is based on reality and immediate experience. The Earth supports us, Water flows, Fire burns, Air circulates. Ancient wisdom thus divided the world into basic elements. These theories of cosmogony, from the Chinese *Yi-King* to Ancient Greece, are all based on the four elements, Earth, Fire, Water, and Air: they are the origin of all living things and of everything that develops, changes, dies, and is reborn. Cold and humidity produce Water; heat and humidity produce Air; heat and dryness, Fire; cold and dryness, Earth. Nature appears to be based on this quadruple principle, symbolically represented by the square: spring, summer, fall, winter; morning, noon, evening, night.

The four elements inspired the four astrological triangles, the representation of which dates back to the Middle Ages *(figure 1)*. At that time, tradition associated mythical character traits with each: Fire was *furious*, Water was *lazy*, Air was *reckless*, and Earth was *melancholy*. The representation of the fifth sign, the World, combined the Earth-sky duality with the four elements. The Star of David, or Solomon's Seal, can be seen here *(figure 2)*.

Figure 2: The World.

The elements are also featured in the form of circles. Fire evoked the sun and Water, reflection. The central point of the circle recalled the invisible aspect of the Air. The Earth was divided into four, like the four seasons or the four corners of the Earth. In figure 4, the World, the symbolism of the cross has several meanings, including the active and passive principles and the opposition of Earth and sky; the cross also summarizes the four cardinal points and evokes the human figure *(figures 3 and 4)*.

Figure 3: Fire, Water, Air, Earth.

Figure 1: Fire, Water, Air, Earth.

Figure 4: The World.

The four elements and the signs of the zodiac. Undated.

It is interesting to compare these representations with those of alchemy, because they intersect and interpenetrate. For instance, Water in alchemy becomes Aquarius in astrology. The alchemistic Spirit of Scales or Balance becomes Libra (*figures 5 and 6*).

Figure 5: Water.

Figure 6: Spirit.

WATER

This is the universal matrix—the ocean, rainwater, plasma, blood, sap. It represents the original medium which mixes, impregnates and assimilates. Water is unstable by definition, it is all receptivity and passivity, a binding and retaining agent, a mobile, plastic and impressionable element. Astrology associates the lymphatic temperament with it, the vegetative state, and sleep. The morphology of the Water type is dilated. Water evokes memory, habit, and the preservation instinct. It covers such vast areas as the unconscious, the imagination, dreams, contemplation and sensitivity. From fantasy through confusion, the Water signs are *Cancer*, *Scorpio*, and *Pisces*.

AIR

Air represents the gaseous state, in relation to diffusion and expansion. It is light, volatile, enveloping and exposed to all contacts, travel and movement, evoking freedom and availability. The Air evokes a world of mixed influences and combination, animation and exchange; it is humid and hot. It is an agent of linkage, associated with a sanguine temperament and marked by the predominance of the respiratory function, blood circulation and sexual activity. Astrology attributes a dilated and tonic morphology to it, a lively appetite for life and demanding sensory desires. The Air temperament is expansive; it vibrates and adapts spontaneously, loves parties and romance, embraces existence with enthusiasm and delight. From exchange through sublimation, the Air signs are *Gemini*, *Libra*, and *Aquarius*.

FIRE

Fire recreates and transforms matter, consumes or destroys it. It isolates, exalts and intensifies everything it touches, sometimes purifying, sometimes aggressive. The Fire of maturity embellishes and appeases, the Fire of the desert dries and sterilizes. It is a factor in struggle and progress, exceeding and affirming. Fire is associated with action and war, energy and retraction. It is associated with a bilious and muscular temperament, the functions of reactivity and leadership. It cannot be dissociated from conquest—of the world or of inner conquest—from passion and domination. Astrology attributes dynamic qualities to Fire, those aimed at consciousness and elevation. From excitation through consummation, the Fire signs are *Aries*, *Leo*, and *Sagittarius*.

EARTH

The Earth represents a state of condensation and concentration of matter which it aims to preserve and reduce. This element's appearance is dry and cold, and it defines, fixes and mineralizes objects and bodies on which it imposes first materialization, and subsequently putrefaction. The Earth nourishes, resists and consolidates but it also plunders and buries. It is the instinctive element *par excellence*, that of limitations and geometric figures. In astrology, this element is associated with a down-to-earth, nervous and introverted temperament. This type of person has a retracted morphology, and his rich, profound and complex existence will gradually lead him down the path of abstraction. From density through fossilization, the Earth signs are *Taurus*, *Virgo*, and *Capricorn*.

FIRST IMPRESSIONS

A study of a chart of the Heavens will give an initial impression of harmony. The chart appears to be balanced if it shows an even distribution of the various elements over the zodiac and the presence of the four elements, Earth, Air, Water, and Fire. It may appear unbalanced, however, if there is a concentration of elements in one hemisphere, one or more signs crowded together, or the absence of one or more elements. These first indications are valuable as they immediately show where a problem may lie. The lack of Fire is interpreted as a difficulty in putting words into deeds, an excess of Water of being over-emotional. The absence of Air shows difficulty in communicating. The absence of or an excessive amount of Earth can be viewed as a conflict between the innate and reality.

THE ASTROLABE

THE CELESTIAL SPHERE

IN THE DISTANT PAST, THE CHALDEAN AND EGYPTIAN PRIESTS WERE ABLE TO DETERMINE THE LENGTH OF THE SOLAR YEAR AND forecast when an eclipse would take place. Astrology was born out of ancient rites of the people mixed with magic. It spread through the lands later conquered by Islam, from Indonesia to the shores of the Mediterranean. During the reign of Alexander the Great (336–323 B.C.), it reached Greece before influencing ancient Rome. About a hundred and forty years before Christ, Hipparchus, one of the founders of Greek astronomy, measured the length of the tropical year and drew up the first sun tables. Nearly three centuries later, Ptolemy produced the canon of Hellenistic astrology, entitled *Tetrabiblos*. The Arabs took advantage of these discoveries, encouraged by great caliphs such as Al-Mansur and Al-Mamoon. Thus, in 975, the Persian astronomer, Omar Sheyan, reorganized the calendar by introducing bissextile years. In the early Middle Ages, Greco-Arab astronomy was re-introduced into Europe by the monk Gerbert d'Aurillac (938–1003), who became pope under the name of Sylvester II. In Spain, astrology found an ardent defender in King Alphonso X of Castile, nicknamed "the Astrologer."

Astrolabes, which had been used by astronomers since Antiquity, were used to determine the height of the stars above the horizon. These were not only instruments of precision but also elegant art objects which provided evidence of advanced trigonometric knowledge. With regard to cosmology, certain definitions date back to long ago, sometimes even well before the common era.

The apparent path of the sun was given the name *ecliptic* by the Greeks. It is to Aristotle (384–322 B.C.) that we owe the term *zodiac*, meaning "concerning animals." The zodiac is a ring of sky containing constellations in the shape of animals and extending eight degrees on either side of the ecliptic. Seen from the Earth, the planets seem to move within the zodiac. To understand their position, one needs to imagine the celestial sphere as an extension of the earthly sphere. *The celestial equator* bisects the ecliptic at two points, one of which, the *vernal point*, corresponds to the spring or vernal equinox. Western astrology, based on the Greco-Arab tradition, is, in fact, tropical, that is to say, it is based on the return of the sun to the vernal point. The phenomenon of the *precession of the equinoxes* was discovered by Hipparchus in ancient times. At the time, the sun appeared to be in the constellation of Aries between March 21 and April 21. Due to the Earth's inclination on its axis, the sun moves into a new sign about every 2,000 years. That is why the sun is no longer in the same position in relation to the constellations.

Previous page: symbolic representation of the overthrow of the vision of the Earth in the Universe. Woodcut, 1888.
Facing: "Mother" astrolabe (Iraq, 1306), with added "Spider" astrolabe (Turkey, 1685.)

SIGNS OF THE ZODIAC

THE RHYTHM OF THE COSMOS

THE ZODIAC, THE PART OF THE SKY FILLED WITH CONSTELLATIONS, REPRESENTS THE APPARENT PATH TRAVELED BY THE SUN. THE ZODIAC IS divided into twelve signs of thirty degrees each, in each of which the sun appears to linger for about a month. Aries, the Ram, the first sign of the zodiac, corresponds to the *vernal point* and the vernal or spring equinox.

It should be emphasized that Western astrology does not take the constellations themselves into account, but merely borrows their names and their mythologies, the origins of which have been lost in the mists of time. The constellation of Leo, the Lion, is, in any case, the only one to bear any resemblance to its name. Some of the names may be linked to seasonal work, among them Virgo, the virgin, for harvesting, and Pisces, the fish, for fishing, and so on.

It is hard to determine whether the mythologies linked to the constellations were inspired by observed characteristics or the reverse. Some writers, including Rupert Gleadow, consider that "the signs received their symbolic names from the influxes which were discovered for them and these names were then attached to the constellations" (*Astrology in Everyday Life*, 1940).

At the human level, the zodiac translates itself into character traits based on primary characteristics from the basic impulses of Aries the Ram to the final dilution of Pisces the Fish.

The twelve signs are divided into two cycles of six. These are the *introverted cycle*, which are turned inward, from Aries to Virgo and the *extroverted cycle*, turned outward to others, from Libra to Pisces.

CARDINAL SIGNS, FIXED SIGNS, AND MUTABLE SIGNS

The signs are traditionally classified into three distinct categories. The cardinal signs are at the beginning of the season, the fixed signs are in the middle, and the mutable or changeable signs come at the end.

Cardinal signs:
- Aries (spring)
- Cancer (summer)
- Libra (fall)
- Capricorn (winter)

These signs are fleeting, impetuous and hasty. Whatever they do, they do better at first.

Fixed signs:
- Taurus (spring)
- Leo (summer)
- Scorpio (fall)
- Aquarius (winter)

These signs are firm and resistant, showing authority and a certain amount of obstinacy in their actions.

Facing and following page: contemporary reproduction of the twelve signs of the zodiac by Herrad von Landsperg, from Hortus Deliciarum (destroyed in a fire.) 12th century.

Mutable signs:

-Gemini (spring)

-Virgo (summer)

-Sagittarius (fall)

-Pisces (winter)

These signs are changeable and versatile, easily attracted by novelty.

THE HEMISPHERES

Depending on the time of year, from a geocentric point of view, the map of the sky appears to be divided into four distinct hemispheres, each of which may contain any number of planets at a given time.

The Eastern Hemisphere, in the left section of the map of the sky, concerns the eastern part of the local Heaven. The planets rise in this part of the sky. If this hemisphere is dominant, the cosmic climate favors independence, authority, courage, responsibility, and dynamism. The corollaries are solitude and egocentrism.

The Western Hemisphere, which is on the right when looking at a map of the Heavens, covers the western part of the local sky. In this hemisphere, the planets are waning. When this hemisphere is dominant, the cosmic climate gains in adaptability, diplomacy, and humanity. It may also sometimes incline toward opportunism and conventionality.

The diurnal hemisphere, which is above the horizon, concerns the visible part of the local sky. The planets are visible here. If this hemisphere is dominant, the cosmos tends toward personal affirmation, favoring image and outward show, and even exhibitionism.

The nocturnal hemisphere below the horizon covers the invisible part of the local sky. The influence of the planets is reduced because it is blocked by the Earth. When this hemisphere is dominant, the cosmos favors intuition, philosophical judgment, thought and meditation and may tend toward submission and materialism.

THE AGE OF AQUARIUS

The Age of Aquarius has been announced as a golden age. When will it begin? Some astronomers situate it in about 2160, others believe it has already begun. Since the Earth is inclined on its axis, the 0° Aries will soon correspond to the 30° Aquarius. Each astrological age covers a period of about two thousand years. The Age of Pisces coincided with the advent of the great monotheistic religions, ending in the triumph of science and materialism. Humanism and the fraternity of Aquarius will soon cause today's materialism to be replaced by a search for new spiritual values. The new age is presaged in the growth of communications and the conquest of space.

ARIES

March 21 - April 21
Element: Fire
Dominant planet: Mars

THE RAM IS THE ARDENT HERALD OF SPRING. LIFE BEGINS AGAIN AFTER THE DORMANT WINTER AND BURSTS FORTH IN ALL ITS glory. This fanfare of rebirth is evocative of the cry of the newborn baby. The sign begins at the moment of the equinox and restores the balance between day and night. As it progresses, the days grow longer.

Aries the Ram contributes the vital Fire which coincides with the return of the light but corresponds to the aggressive nature of Mars, its planet, traditionally associated with violence and cruelty. The Ram breaks through and shows the way, but the way is often one of confrontation. As the first sign of the zodiac, it has the attributes and defects of the eldest—authority, courage, and leadership, but a violence and impulsiveness which cause it to be rebellious and trouble-making.

The sign of Aries evokes the Ram and it is no accident that the Ancients chose this symbol to represent a lively and impatient nature. The ideogram evokes maleness, the leader of the flock. The reductive symbolism—the ram's horns to represent the whole animal—is a reminder that the head is the part of the body associated with the Ram. Other senses result from it: the drawing also represents a battering ram, the ancient instrument of war consisting of a beam ending in a head and used in battle to break down walls. The idea of war is dominant, as is that of breaking open. The graphic also shows an arch of folded leaves and a shoot emerging from the Earth, the symbol of birth and initiation.

MYTHOLOGY

The Ram often appears as a variation on the Lamb of God which offers itself as a sacrifice as a salvation for sinners. This meaning is reinforced by the etymology of the words *agni* (primordial fire) and *agnus* (lamb, the Lamb of God).

This theme occurs in the myth of Jason. Jason was a young king without a crown and was forced to bring back the Golden Fleece, shorn from a mythical ram, which was guarded by a dragon. Instead of confronting the monster, he resorted to the magical potions of his wife, the sorceress Medea. He put the dragon to sleep and made off with the Fleece. This trickery did not prevent his kingdom and life from falling into chaos. Medea fled, after cutting her childrens' throats. The parable illustrates the search for power and immortality, symbolized by the Golden Fleece. The dragon represents perverse desire, glory, and vanity, which must be overcome. The Ram incarnates the initiation into the higher truths which man must deserve. This was not the case with Jason, who was too eager to justify his life by a half-finished exploit.

Facing and following pages: the signs of the zodiac. French illuminations, circa 1423.

TAURUS

April 22 - May 21
Element: Earth
Dominant planets: Venus and the moon

TAURUS, THE BULL, ILLUSTRATES THE FLOW-ERING OF SPRING. AS THE SECOND SIGN OF THE ZODIAC IT CELEBRATES THE MILDNESS of the climate and the generosity of nature. In Upper Egypt, the year began with the new moon in Taurus, as an indication of fertility. The bull's horn, like the crescent moon, is a symbol of abundance. The Earth, the element on which it rests summarizes the Taurean philosophy.

The Bull looks for stability, anchored in reality. Action for its own sake is of no interest to it, if it is not linked to a concrete objective. Creativity is not its priority, but it knows how to make the best of its gifts by working methodically.

The sign evokes the axle of the wheel on which the carriage of society rests. It must remain steady. The Bull appreciates routine and is wary of improvisation. It likes comfort, is slow-moving, mulling over ideas and decisions. It takes time to get started but is not easily discouraged.

The ideogram evokes an animal with a sensual and prolific temperament. The bull, whose worship involves many sacrificial rites, symbolizes spiritual initiation in this context.

On the astrological level, this ideogram can be read in several ways. It can be imagined to represent the soil subjected to the rays of the moon suggested by the crescent. Or one can see the solar disk combined with the crescent moon, the union of the masculine and feminine principles. Finally, the ideogram also shows the egg of the world supporting the cup from which it receives life. This definition is the translation of the receptivity of the sign and its long memory.

MYTHOLOGY

In most traditions, the bull represents the baser, as opposed to the divine, instincts of the animal. The bullfight, in which the beast is slowly put to death, recalls ancient sacrifices and initiation rites. Man celebrates the triumph of intellect over brute force, at least in theory.

In mythology, the winged bull who seduced the nymph Europa was probably inspired by Nandi, Shiva's white bull. Jupiter took on the form of this magical animal to win the heart of the woman he coveted. The nymph, Europa, caressed the bull's hide, then climbed on his back and he carried her away as far as the island of Crete. There, the god resumed his normal shape and had congress with her. He commemorated the exploit by putting the remains of the animal in the sky, where it produced the constellation of Taurus. As with all myths, this one contains a grain of wisdom: the handsome, white, winged animal symbolizes fertility and incarnates sexual energy. Riding the Bull is equivalent to mastering it, transforming its sexual power into spiritual energy.

GEMINI

May 22 - June 21
Element: Air
Dominant planet: Mercury

GEMINI, THE TWINS, MARK THE END OF SPRING. THEY CELEBRATE THE GAIETY OF JUNE, AND THE OPTIMISM OF NATURE. THE PREVIOUS signs are more instinctive and are represented by animals. Gemini has a human configuration. The Air, its element, confers lightness, elevation, and a talent for communication. Duality reinforces these qualities. A Gemini is often split between taking two contrary paths, though this internal debate does not prevent him from taking action.

The sign is governed by Mercury, a planet of the mind. It plays the same role in the zodiac as does the nervous system in the human body. It is an agent of transmission, with a predisposition for interpretation, teaching and trade, all activities ruled by Mercury. This sign possesses the seductions of adolescence. Fascinated by novelty, Gemini retains an inexhaustible fountain of youth. He or she has a few principles but no strict rules. The need for companionship lends them to be social animals, good at team games.

Gemini is one of the three human signs of the zodiac; the others are Virgo and Aquarius. The ideogram illustrates the superiority of intellect over instinct in its representation of Castor and Pollux, the Heavenly Twins, in their fraternal complimentarity. Theirs is a duality of spirit and matter. In the zodiac, Gemini represents the initial awakening of consciousness, the vertical lines symbolizing the spirit and the horizontal lines, substance.

A similar meaning attributes the undifferentiated energies of the two previous signs, Aries and Taurus, to the vertical lines which are combined to form the first step in individualization. These interpretations combine to evoke the spirit of fraternity, the indispensable mortar for any human construction, in any civilization.

MYTHOLOGY

Castor and Pollux were an unusual pair. Their mother, Leda, conceived the former with a mortal, but Pollux was the seed of Jupiter. One brandished a lyre, the other a club. Intrepid, and always ready to play a dirty trick, the twins abducted two young girls from under the noses of their fiancés. Castor lost his life. Pollux was so inconsolable that Jupiter, his father, struck a bargain with him. Since Pollux agreed to share his immortality with his brother, they would henceforth spend half their time on Earth and the rest in Olympus. In this story, Castor symbolizes instinct, Pollux, the divine spark which guides human beings in their development. The sacrifice of the more primitive side of human nature enables the heroes to reconquer Eden. The Twins thus contributed to redeeming man from his original fall and restored his dignity as a demi-god.

CANCER

June 22 - July 22
Element: Water
Dominant planet: the moon

THE FOURTH SIGN STARTS AT THE SUMMER SOLSTICE ON MID-SUMMER'S EVE, A PROPITIOUS DATE FOR THE SABBATH, FAIRIES AND MAGIC spells. The summer is at its height, flowers and fruit are abundant, nature celebrates its fecundity as well as dreams and imagination. Its element is Water, receptive and moving, which evokes mother's milk, the sap rising in the trees, the ocean and rain. The moon, close yet mysterious, is a cycle symbolizing everlasting return. It harbors sensitive, changing values as well as an apparent passivity which hides its effervescent interior life and creative powers.

Life, for a Cancerian, resembles a waking dream, which is clear and confused by turns because reason remains a stranger to him or her and he or she is guided by intuition like a sixth sense. They live by emotion and memory, sheltered from the outside world within the warmth of a cocoon.

The ideogram of the sign, two intertwined spirals, expresses the change in the direction in which the sun travels after the summer solstice. From being in the ascendant, it starts to descend. The liquid element is suggested by the wavy lines—the waves of life. The shape of an egg, a closed world, the union of body and spirit, and the process of gestation in preparation for birth, can also be discerned.

This protected space evokes the alchemist's crucible in which activity must remain secret. It thus expresses the contrast between apparent passivity and the intense interior activity of a Cancerian.

MYTHOLOGY

Mythology frequently refers to the powers of the moon, the changing divinity which reigns over the shadows. The Ancients already venerated its influence over births and harvests, but another aspect of its myth is more specifically connected with Cancer, the crab. The moon appears here as the *Casta Diva*, the untouchable goddess personified in many stories as the huntress Diana, or as Hecate.

Diana, who hunted with silver arrows, lived chastely surrounded by nymphs and punished any assault on her dignity with death. Hecate has three faces and waits at the crossroads, the mistress of sorcery. These malevolent creatures have become cruel through sexual frustration. The myth of Selene is slightly pleasanter, although surrounded by mystery. The beautiful goddess falls in love at first sight with the shepherd Endymion and puts him into an eternal sleep. This magic sleep illustrates the hypnotic character of the moon, its possessiveness and modesty.

LEO

July 23 - August 23
Element: Fire
Dominant planet: the Sun

LEO, THE LION, DOMINATES HIGH SUMMER. AS THE FIFTH SIGN (FIVE IS THE SYMBOL OF PERFECTION), IT MARKS A HIGH POINT IN THE cycle of the seasons. The Fire of the Lion is a powerful but controlled element, a leap into spirituality. Astrology associates this sign with the sun, the centre of the Universe, and with gold, the sun of metals. The Lion is a very common symbol of sovereignty and divine power, evoking the renewal of cosmic energy and the victory of day over night. In this respect, it is also an image of resurrection. The Lion irradiates and possesses a natural ascendancy over others. Leos give themselves ambitious goals and need to live in a heroic dimension. Are they able to enlighten those who approach them and reveal them to themselves? Through its own flowering, the sign can reveal its grandeur. Even though it occupies centre stage, it does not try to steal the limelight but merely to dispense it generously.

The two principles represented in Cancer, the previous sign, are combined in Leo to make a single, unique and majestic one. The birth is accomplished, giving rise to the Ego. The graphic of the sign evokes its proud definition. The large loop suggests the aristocracy of the sun and radiant expansion from the centre.

MYTHOLOGY

The lion of Nemaea, a little town in ancient Greece, was reputed to be invincible. Hercules covered himself with its skin after finally beating it, thus materializing its magic aura. This spoil, the symbol of a glory acquired at a great price, became the mask behind which he could shelter—his *persona*. In Greek mythology, Apollo, god of the silver arch, represents the sun crossing the sky in his magnificent chariot. Apollo had one great asset, his athletic body, but his vanity made his relationships explosive ones. He suffered many rebuffs, including that of the prophetess Cassandra. Out of spite, he cast a spell whereby no one would ever believe her predictions. During a tournament, Apollo accidentally killed his lover Hyacynthos—a hyacinth bloomed from his blood. However, the god was loved by nymphs and had many sons, including the enigmatic Orpheus, the prince of magicians.

Beyond his superficial physical perfection, Apollo is the symbol of elevation. His beauty arouses human desire and does not seek to extinguish but rather to domesticate. His own excesses have taught him wisdom; the work he has done on himself celebrates the victory of the spirit. He is a saver of souls, a moralist in his own way, who first defends his personal ethic. As a healer and conductor of the muses, Apollo is the model of civilization itself. The Ancients awarded him the laurel wreath.

VIRGO

August 24 - September 23
Element: Earth
Dominant planet: Mercury

AFTER THE SPLENDOR OF LEO, VIRGO MARKS A RETURN TO INTROVERSION. SHE COUNTERS THE VALUES OF HEAT AND EXUBERANCE WITH cool reserve. It is harvest time, the days are getting shorter and encourage foresight. Her attitude is one of discipline and organization. Her element, the Earth, has produced fruit and is awaiting a new cycle in order to regenerate itself. The Earth is here an element of stability through which the Virgin acquires a measure of security. Mercury, her planet, symbolizes order and care—it features in the caduceus of physicians and nurses. Virgoans study and analyze in order to come to a logical conclusion. Virgo is humble and modest, developing from insecurity to a feeling of inferiority because this critical spirit is applied to everything. The Virgin has no desire to prove herself, she prefers to save herself. This prudence and caution are both her weakness, preventing her from aiming high and achieving her ambitions, and her strength, because they mould her into an effective and brave character.

The ideogram of the sign represents an M with a fourth folded leg. It can be interpreted as a winged virgin holding an ear of wheat. The M refers to the maternal principle personified in mythology in the form of Demeter. There is no aggression in her. The folding of the letter evokes the predominance of the material world. In the curlicues and folds of the graphic, some authors perceive a reminder of the digestive system, which is linked to this sign.

MYTHOLOGY

Mythology is ambiguous in the case of Virgo. The legend which surrounds her brings together a strange trio, consisting of Persephone and her mother Demeter, both goddesses of the harvest, and Pluto (Hades), the god of Hell. Pluto wanted to marry Persephone, but her mother rejected him. He therefore carried off the daughter to his kingdom where he married her and proclaimed her Queen of the Dead. The frantic mother pursued him relentlessly, moving Heaven and Earth, and finally found her daughter. But the young queen liked her new home and broke her sacred fast. Jupiter (Zeus), her father, rendered judgment. Persephone could live in Hell with her husband for six months, but must return to Olympus to spend the summer with her mother and the other divinities.

This tale illustrates the way in which life and death are inseparable. The girl discovered love at the very moment that she penetrated the kingdom of the shadows. There is a hint of the rites of resurrection, the Mysteries of Eleusis. The concluding judgment reflects the ambiguity of the sign. The wise Virgin is Demeter and the foolish Virgin, Persephone; the former weeps while the latter smiles discreetly.

LIBRA

September 24 - October 22
Element: Air
Dominant planet: Venus

LIBRA BEGINS WITH THE FALL EQUINOX AND SYMBOLIZES THE SEASON IN ITS LAVISH YET NOSTALGIC ASPECT. THIS AIR SIGN, WHICH is so taken with beauty, justice, and harmony, indicates a changeable personality, seeking its own equilibrium and oscillating from one mood to another, from one opinion to its opposite. The Air, an active, masculine element, is associated here with Venus and Saturn. It makes Libra into an idealistic sign, full of enthusiasm and excitement, but easily deterred and discouraged. Venus is dedicated to seduction and pleasure. Libra, the Scales, needs to evolve in surroundings of peace and tolerance. Saturn, its other master, confers gravity and rigor on the sign. Behind an apparent superficiality, Librans conceal a deep humanity and demanding ethics. Venus and Saturn define this sign of contradictions, in which light and shade, sensuality and detachment confront each other.

The ideogram first indicates the scales which Libra represents. The straight line indicates balance, the upper line the oscillation of the weighing scales. There is a setting sun on the line of the horizon, because Libra is at dusk in the zodiac. The ideogram also evokes restrained breathing. The complete respiratory cycle is represented in the Air signs—inhalation in Gemini, retention in Libra, and exhalation in Aquarius.

MYTHOLOGY

The myths surrounding Libra are those of Venus which illustrate the power of beauty and transform seduction into a deadly weapon. The goddess had taken shelter from the radiance of Psyche. She thus asked her son Eros (Cupid) to kill Psyche. But Eros, the god of Love, succumbed to the charms of the young girl, married her, and went to live with her on a remote island. The vindictive Venus forbade her daughter-in-law to look upon the face of her husband. Psyche broke this taboo and surprised the young god in his sleep. Eros fled, blaming her, and Psyche thus became the slave of Venus, who sent her to Hell to seek an elixir. She then committed another indiscretion by opening the flask, which sent her into a deep sleep. The story ends with Eros, touched by her faithfulness, waking Psyche with a kiss and offering her ambrosia. The couple would thus share immortality, far from the anger of Venus.

In the story, Psyche lost all her objectivity because, according to human law, love is blind. Her passion was so great that it reduced her to slavery. The moral is that carnal love (Eros) and spiritual love (Psyche), after having sought each other for so long on the road to purification, were joined for eternity.

SCORPIO

October 23 - November 22
Element: Water
Dominant planet: Pluto

SCORPIO COINCIDES WITH FALL TAKING HOLD. THE DAYS BECOME SHORTER, THE TREES LOSE THEIR LEAVES, NATURE GRADUALLY FALLS asleep and freezes over. This time of year is when the force of natural destruction, linked to Scorpio, comes into its own. It is a necessary destruction, linked to life, which precedes rebirth. Death and rebirth are reminiscent of the phoenix, the mythical bird which is constantly reborn from the ashes. Water, its element, is feminine and passive. This is the original water of unconscious urges and primitive emotions. The dominant planets are Pluto and Mars. Pluto, god of the Underworld in Antiquity, links the sign to unacknowledged motivation and secret riches. Mars gives the sign its warlike energy. Scorpio thus inherits a difficult nature. Scorpios are said to be violent, jealous, and possessive, but that is a narrow view because their characters are infinitely more complex. They place themselves deliberately outside the rules and only abide by their own personal code of conduct.

The ideogram of the sign first evokes the scorpion, with its articulated body and poisonous dart in its tail. It also relates to the meaning of M, the feminine principle in the matrix. In the zodiac, Scorpio marks the return to the original waters, a return made possible by the aggression of Mars, whose arrow points upward, by a spiritual quest, suffering, and symbolic death.

MYTHOLOGY

The legend of Orion follows the mythology of the sign quite closely. Significantly, Orion was born in the bowels of the Earth, and was a young man of great beauty, who spent his time hunting and courting Merope, to whom he was betrothed. One night, he became drunk and offended her. Oenopion, father of the young girl, begged Dionysos to punish him. Orion lost consciousness and the old man took advantage of the fact to gouge out his eyes. The young man wandered blindly for a long time until an oracle showed him how to regain his sight. Orion decided to wreak vengeance on Oenopion but could not find him. In Crete, he became the companion of Diana, but again made the mistake of offending the goddess. A scorpion appeared, stung him in the heel and killed him. To commemorate him, Jupiter placed the insect and its victim in the sky, where they gave birth to constellations.

The ambivalence of the sign is evident throughout the story, because the hero's courage is tainted with violence and his tenderness spoiled by lust. Diana should be considered an allegory for the human conscience: unless it is treated adequately, it will cause its loss. However, the hero's downfall symbolizes his road to immortality.

SAGITTARIUS

November 23 - December 21
Element : Fire
Dominant planet: Jupiter

AS THE NINTH SIGN OF THE ZODIAC, SAGITTARIUS MARKS A TRANSITION BETWEEN THE TWO COLD SEASONS. THE ARROW SHOT into the sky suggests an appeal to the infinite. Half human, half horse, the mythological Centaur symbolizes the dual nature of Sagittarius, anchored in reality but tending toward spiritual values through an idealistic quest into the realms of the unknown. The sign's element, Fire, is active and purifying. It is also illuminating and gives humans access to sacred knowledge, detaching them from their primitive nature in order to attain a heroic dimension.

Jupiter, the dominant planet, makes Sagittarians good managers. A Sagittarian is at his or her best when confronted with a challenge. They are daring and intrepid and capable of anything. They are also gourmets, loving pleasure and the company of others, and do not surrender themselves to long and complex introspection. They need space, freedom, and light. This emphasis translates into strong ambition and even megalomania. The Sagittarian is conscious of his or her worth and insists on recognition.

The ideogram is generally summarized by the arrow which the archer is releasing. This image naturally evokes the desire for the expansion of the sign, the anticipation of conquests to come and spiritual projection while the crossbar represents the weight of instinct. The arrow also symbolizes intuition and enlightenment—thought that makes light appear.

MYTHOLOGY

With its supernatural nature, the Centaur becomes one of the initiates. The intuition of the horse informs the reason of man and, reciprocally, the human spirit prevents the beast from going astray. The Centaur embodies the impetuosity of desire and sexuality, emphasized by the bow he draws. Tradition places Centaurs in two groups, the tame and the wild. The former are guided by Chiron toward spiritual power, the latter are bestiality incarnate. When Hercules enters the story, Chiron, a hospitable Centaur offers him Apollo's wine. But this delicious drink belongs to all the Centaurs and when they learn about it, they decide to get revenge. A fight ensues, in the course of which Hercules accidentally wounds Chiron, who is known for his wisdom and skill (his name has given rise to the word "surgery".) In order to ease his suffering, Jupiter places his remains in the firmament as the constellation of Sagittarius.

The heady wine which was the subject and cause of the quarrel is representative of the key to a trance of initiation. Chiron evokes active spirituality, and symbolically, the arrow represents the hand.

CAPRICORN

December 22 - January 20
Element: Earth
Dominant planet: Saturn, Mars

CAPRICORN STARTS ON THE WINTER SOLSTICE, THE LONGEST NIGHT OF THE YEAR. THE TENTH SIGN IS LINKED TO THE STRIPPING AWAY OF nature, evoking rigor. The Earth takes on the cold, hard aspect of December, even though it bears within it the seeds of the following spring. Capricorn's vocation is to harbor this seed, keeping it safe for the coming rebirth.

The sign is governed by Saturn, one of the Titans of mythology, and often confused with Cronos, who is associated with Time. Mars, the other dominant, is the god of War. These two influences produce a strong, opinionated character, who leads life at a slow but steady pace. It should be noted, however, that caprice and Capricorn come from the same root. *Capris,* the goat, is the symbol of the sign. A Capricornian is a secretive person whose character is hard to read. They are obstinate but capable of defending their ideas and goals to the bitter end. They concentrate their strength of character on the essentials. Seemingly impenetrable, they are actually deeply emotional.

The ideogram of the sign first evokes the mythical goat with a dolphin's tail which symbolizes the sign. The loops and curlicues symbolize introversion, self-centeredness, and con-centration of the Capricornian universe. The dual goat-dolphin aspect, emerging and submerged, refer to the duality of spirit and matter, the double question mark to time, whether limited or eternal.

MYTHOLOGY

In mythology, Saturn was so overcome with jealousy and fear of losing power that he swallowed his offspring as they were born. His exasperated wife, Rhea, tied a stone in a cloth and offered it to him instead of Jupiter, his newborn son. Then she whisked the child away to Crete, where nymphs hid him in a cave. He was fed with milk from the goat Amalthea, while the Curetes sang to hide his baby cries. When Jupiter attained adulthood, he resolved to supplant his father. He forced him to regurgitate his five brothers as well as the stone which had been substituted for him. The stone stood at Delphi, where it marked the centre of the world. The nanny goat who had nursed him inspired the constellation of Capricorn.

This legend illustrates the insatiable nature of Saturn and his lust for power. The patriarch incarnates a form of rigid conservatism, incapable of adapting to change. The golden age of Rome, when he was the object of worship in a joyful cult, is a sort of parenthesis in his mythology. Saturn soon returned to Olympus, but he had to be defeated so that he could be replaced by Jupiter and the new generation of divinities.

AQUARIUS

January 21 - February 18
Element: Air
Dominant planet: Uranus

AQUARIUS IS THE PENULTIMATE SIGN OF THE ZODIAC AND MARKS A PROFOUND CHANGE. THIS SIGN OF CONTRASTS IS DISTINGUISHED by its humanity and fraternity. It appears to be fragile but in fact it has great vitality. Winter covers the Earth with an icy mantle while Nature silently prepares to burst forth. Aquarius lends the coldest months its reserve and distance. The Aquarian element is Air, the vector of communication, exhalation and spirituality. In this case, it expresses the purifying essence of the cosmic breath. Uranus, its dominant, encourages Aquarians to break the rules and extend their field of consciousness to acquire a universal vision. Saturn, the other master, confers gravity and seriousness. Naturally appealing, Aquarians do not have to try hard to be liked. Their progressive ideas and generosity make them popular. Both caring and visionary, they have a taste for daring ideas and are always ready to help the underdog.

The heavenly cupbearer pouring his precious liquid over the Earth is one of the three signs represented by a human figure (the others are Gemini and Virgo). Aquarius is an indication of change. Its ideogram is reminiscent of the Egyptian hieroglyph for water, a symbolic water which expresses peace and light. The undulating nature of communication between sky and Earth is suggested by the superimposed wavy lines. In the process of breathing, Aquarius represents the exhalation phase, characterized by the assimilation of spiritual power and a rejection of whatever is unnecessary—in other words, by purification.

MYTHOLOGY

There is a myth about angels in most cultural traditions. According to Nordic legend, the sky owes its azure color to the host of blue angels that inhabit it. The story of Ganymede, the celestial cupbearer, is a slightly romanticized version of this myth. This incredibly handsome young man began by provoking a war between his father and the King of Lydia. He was eventually noticed by Jupiter (Zeus), who abducted him, transformed him into a sacred eagle for the purpose, and transported him to the kingdom of the gods. He was then granted the privilege of serving the gods ambrosia, the precious elixir of immortality. Jupiter made Ganymede his lover before fixing him in the firmament as Aquarius, not far from the constellation of the Eagle. The story illustrates the universality of beauty, regardless of sex. The cupbearer's amphora pours the water of knowledge on future generations.

PISCES

February 19 - March 20
Element: Water
Dominant planet: Neptune

PISCES, THE TWELFTH AND LAST SIGN OF THE ZODIAC, MARKS THE END OF THE ANNUAL CYCLE. THIS STAGE OF DISSOLVING PRECEDES rebirth. The sign is associated with water, with rivers in spate and melting snows, the synonym of submerging and regeneration. Neptune, god of the oceans and symbol of the imagination, confers great psychic powers and a strong sixth sense upon those born under this sign. Pisceans can detect beyond appearances. This internal richness can be an asset or a weakness, depending on whether they build on it or are overcome by it. Jupiter offers them his expansiveness and Venus her sensuality. Pisceans are sociable and altruistic, love festivities and earthly pleasures. But they are ambiguous, as quick to close in upon themselves as to give of themselves. Even though they are outgoing, they are also introspective. Only a higher ideal, whether philosophical or religious, can manage to extract them from their contradictions and the troubled waters in which they navigate.

Pisces is a Water sign, linked to the wettest time of year, and is represented by two semi-circles linked by a crossbar. This ideogram represents the dual polarity of the sign, one turned to the inner world, the other toward the collective adventure. It symbolizes the ambivalence of the sign, which goes in two opposite directions. The left-hand semi-circle which dates back to the Flood can be interpreted as the end of a world, and the right-hand one as the beginning of the next. The crossbar represents a transition—Noah's ark. Pisces thus indicates the interim between two cosmic eras.

MYTHOLOGY

Mythology contains many stories of Neptune's disputes with other aquatic divinities. Typhon, the foaming monster, vowed to defeat the gods. After fighting Jupiter, he pursued Venus in his fury. The goddess of love did not know how to escape him and plunged into the sea in desperation. Neptune sent a pair of dolphins to bring her back to terra firma. As a gesture of gratitude for their assistance, Jupiter placed the dolphins in the firmament, where they gave birth to the constellation of Pisces.

In the story, Venus, born from the foam of the waves, returns to her original element. But for this proud seductress, the watery environment represents a regression. Her flight reveals the inadequacy of her weapons. What can love do when faced with brute force? Venus was saved in the end, however, because love conquers all. That is Christ's teaching: the first Christians used the fish as the symbol of salvation in recognition of this fact. Thus, Pisceans have the role of saviors.

THE PLANETS

WANDERERS IN THE SKY

SINCE THE EARLIEST TIMES, MAN HAS IMAGINED A PARALLEL BETWEEN THE CELESTIAL ORDER AND THE TERRESTRIAL ORDER. THAT IS how the symbolism of the planets (or "wanderers," from the Greek *errantes*) was born, assuming a special relationship between the course of the planets and the destiny of man. The theory of "the unity of things" was disputed by rationalists and was supported by the idea of synchronicity formulated by Carl Gustav Jung. "Synchronicity," he wrote, "is the simultaneous occurrence of two events linked by meaning rather than by cause." (*Synchronicity: An Acausal Connecting Principle*.) Astrology is thus the art of interpreting coincidences between the microcosm and the macrocosm. This symbolism has since been confirmed mathematically. In the 1960s, Michel Gauquelin, a French psychologist and mathematician, subjected astrology to a calculation of probabilities. According to his samples, the planet Mars appears to be close to the highest point in the sky in the chart of policemen and soldiers, Jupiter in that of actors and politicians, and so forth. Recent work done by a French team of researchers, the RAMS (Astrological Research by Scientific Methods) appear to confirm his conclusions.

In the *Tetrabiblos*, which dates back to the second century A.D., Ptolemy refers to the seven planets known to the ancient world: the sun, the moon, Mercury, Venus, Mars, Jupiter, and Saturn. Each planet had an influence on human beings.

The seven planets corresponded to the seven Heavens, the seven days of the week, the seven states or operations of the soul, the seven theological or moral virtues, the seven metals, and so on. The *Kabbalah,* written in the Middle Ages, correlates all parts of the Universe with human traditions and establishes a relationship between the *spheres,* or planets, in the ancient meaning of the word, and the *angels* and their *cosmic function.* The archangel Michael is associated with the sun (the light of the world), Gabriel with the moon (giver of the force of hope and dreams), Mercury with Raphael (the civilizer), Venus with Amael (the lover), Mars with Samael (the destroyer), Jupiter with Zachariel (the organizer) and Saturn with Oriphiel (the watcher). This symbolism is directly inspired by astrology.

It was not until 1781 that the British astronomer, William Herschel, discovered an eighth planet, Uranus. An attractive astrological theory associates the discovery of a planet with its own period of influence. Uranus is thus linked to the French Revolution. Neptune, which was first observed in 1846, corresponds to another historic date, the Revolution of 1848, a socialist revolution which was followed by "the people's spring." The discovery of Pluto, in 1930, coincides with Freud's work on the unconscious. According to certain documents, such as the Aztec calendars, two more planets remain to be discovered, Vulcan and Proserpina. In any event, their period of influence has not yet begun.

Facing page: representation of the planet Earth.
Illumination from the Livre de la propriété des choses, *Bartholomeus Anglicus. 15th century.*

THE PLANETARY ASPECTS

The perpetual movement of the planets draws variable angles in the cosmos, ranging from 0° to 360°. These are traditionally known as *aspects* and are accorded a special significance.

Conjunction (0°–17°) is a powerful aspect that brings two or more planets into contact with each other whose symbolism is mutually enriching, like two people living under the same roof.

Opposition (180° ± 17°) implies duality. This relationship expresses contrast and complementarity. The sun/moon opposition to the full moon, for example, exacerbates the attributes and defects of both these light-givers.

The *square* (90° ± 5°) repeats the symbolism of the number 4, which expresses a construction, a structured activity. It is a dynamic, but often uncomfortable, angle.

The *trine* (120° ± 5°) is taken from the symbolism of the number 3, which evokes communication and associations of the mind. It links two signs in the same element whose modes of operation are complementary.

The *sextile* (60° ± 4°) is taken from the symbolism of the number 6 and expresses practical organization. It is a harmonious aspect which links two complementary elements, Fire and Air, or Earth and Water, but which sometimes produces delays in action.

There are three minor aspects, the *half-square* (45°), the *semi-sextile* (30°) and the *quincunx* (150°), which have a slight effect upon the planets. Some authors also talk of planets being "at war" with each other when they occupy the same degree. Whichever planet has the shortest longtitude is said to win the war.

THE SUN

THE SUN IS PHYSICALLY A VERY BRILLIANT STAR, WHOSE DIAMETER IS MORE THAN A HUNDRED TIMES GREATER THAN THAT OF the Earth. It is surrounded by the planets, which travel in elliptical orbits around it. The sun is almost spherical and produces and emits energy. The solar system is part of a galaxy whose visible trace is called the Milky Way. For the Ancients, the Milky Way represented a drop of milk which escaped from Juno's breast while she was feeding Hercules. It is actually an accumulation of stars. In the late eighteenth century, English astronomer William Herschel produced the first theory that all stars were grouped together into a huge mass. They constituted a disk-shaped structure, which was slightly swollen in the centre and divided into spiral arms. This formation was named a galaxy from the Greek word for "milk," *gala*, inspired by its whitish look. Our solar system is at the edge of the Milky Way, at the end of one of the arms. The Milky Way makes the complete tour of the celestial sphere. Despite its distance of more than 93 million miles from the Earth, the sun's light takes only eight minutes to reach us.

The sun is not only at the heart of the solar system, but it is the source of all life. It irradiates a light which the other planets reflect and keeps them in their respective positions in the system.

Sun worship has been practiced at various times in history. The sun was venerated and feared as an independent god in the Aztec civilization. Four thousand years ago in Egypt, King Akhenaton tried to replace polytheism with a monotheistic religion dedicated to the god Ra. The Romans at the time of the decline of the empire proclaimed the sun the supreme god of the Capitol. In Greek mythology, the sun is associated with the legend of Apollo, the god of agriculture and the seasons, vanquisher of the serpent which symbolized the evils of winter. His oracles were issued by the pythoness at Delphi.

Since Ptolemy (second century A.D.), astrology has attributed vision, brainpower, nerves and the organs on the right side of the body to the sun—not forgetting the third finger of the hand. Its metal is gold, its animal the lion, its flower the heliotrope, and its day of the week Sunday.

ELEMENT: Fire.

TIME OF LIFE: adulthood.

PRINCIPLE: creation, idealism.

PSYCHOLOGY: conscience, integration, control, sublimation.

OCCUPATIONS: management, administration, creative work.

SYMBOLS: success, reputation, honor, prestige, pride.

CHARACTERS	POSITIVE	NEGATIVE
PERSONAL	Energy, optimism, will, loyalty, frankness, dignity, generosity, independence.	Authoritarianism, egocentrism, megalomania.
SOCIAL	Creativity, vitality, radiance, perfectionism, entrepreneurial spirit, daring.	Dictatorialism, exhibitionism.
EMOTIONAL	A passionate and possessive nature, demonstrative, self-possessed.	Jealousy, over-dramatization.

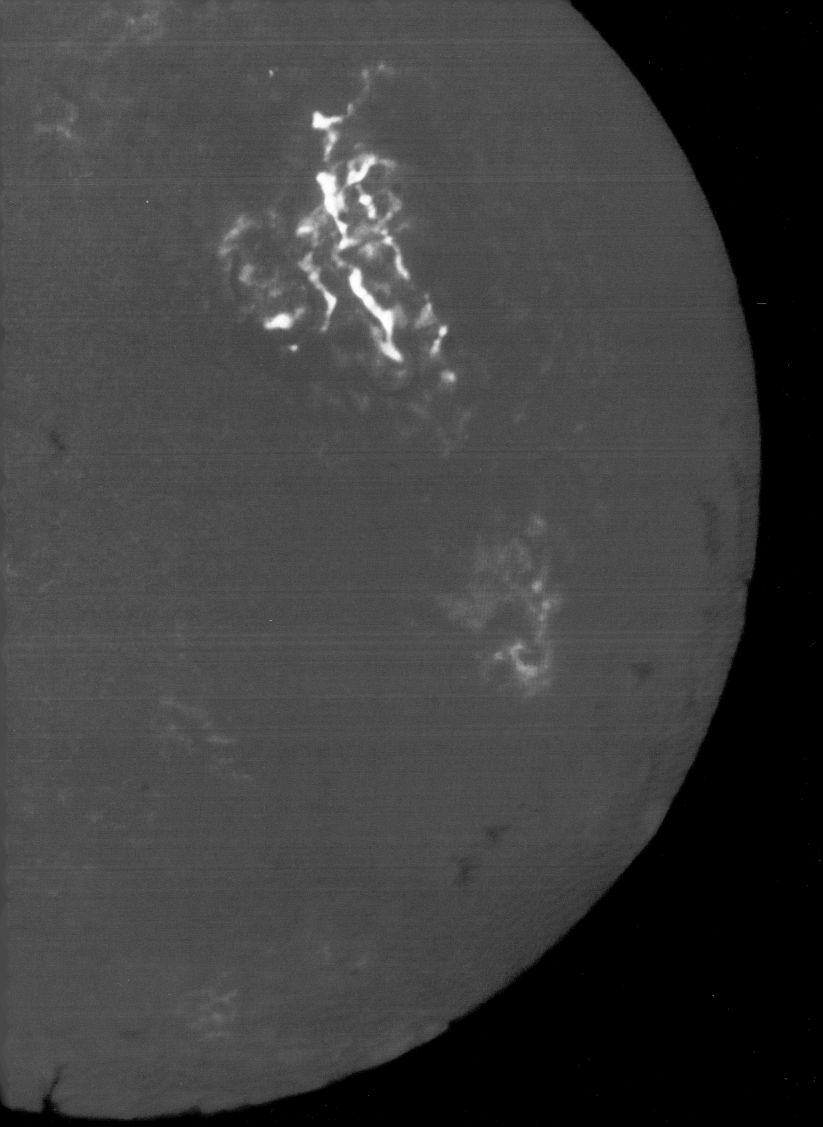

THE MOON

FOR THE MODERN GENERATION, THE MOON IS EARTH'S NATURAL SATELLITE, ON WHICH THE AMERICAN ASTRONAUT NEIL ARMSTRONG first set foot in July 1969. We know that this satellite is small, with a diameter only one quarter that of the Earth. However, its proximity to Earth—only 218,000 miles away—gives it a magnetic influence which is mainly perceptible in the flow of liquids: the ebb and flow of the tides is under its influence combined with that of the sun, and the menstrual cycle of women reproduces the rhythm of the phases of the moon.

Its imprint can be found in the mythology of all ages, and it is always associated with magic. The skulls found in the burial sites of prehistoric caves are arranged to reproduce the disk of the moon. The city of Jericho, founded nine thousand years ago, was dedicated to the moon (its name comes from *Yareah*, "moon" in Semitic languages.) At first it was a masculine entity and inspired the Sin cult in Arabia and that of Osiris in Egypt. Moses himself appears to be a lunar prophet, since his story is rich in symbolic allusions. Mount Sinai refers to *Sin*, the moon. In the Greco-Roman world, the god had an ambiguous connotation. "The mother of the cosmic universe has a nature which is both male and female," observed Plutarch. The cult of Diana-Artemis, the untouchable goddess, corresponds to this definition, as do the goddesses Hecate and Selene. These figures can be beneficent and fertile or malevolent and bringers of death. The moon, which constantly reappears, seems to belong with the shadows. Islam took the crescent moon as its symbol of war; Indian astrology reserves it pride of place in prediction, associating it with the masculine gender. In Western astrology, however, the moon is linked to the feminine principle, with rest, cold and unconscious psychic phenomena. Dreams, primitive impulses, the life of the senses and the fabric of emotion are all within its domain. Its day of the week is Monday.

ELEMENT: Water.

TIME OF LIFE: childhood.

PRINCIPLE: receptivity, plasticity, fertility.

PSYCHOLOGY: gentleness, fantasy, imagination.

OCCUPATIONS: child-rearing, teaching, the arts, public relations, politics.

SYMBOLS: mother, wife, the public.

CHARACTERISTICS	POSITIVE	NEGATIVE
PERSONAL	Intuition, sensitivity, reverie.	Untidiness, susceptibility, over-emotionality, introversion.
SOCIAL	Imagination, inspiration, humor, popularity.	Lethargy, inefficiency, capriciousness.
EMOTIONAL	Attachment to the past, love of art and poetry.	Instability, anger, depression.

THE MOON AMONG THE SIGNS

In Aries:	produces an inflamed imagination and conquering instinct.
In Taurus:	confers femininity and love of nature.
In Gemini:	emphasizes flexibility and plasticity.
In Cancer:	highlights the imaginative and maternal aspects.
In Leo:	produces a colored imagination, magnificence and pride.
In Virgo:	inspires a sense of organization and self-criticism.
In Libra:	develops esthetic sensitivity.
In Scorpio:	inspires delusions and obsessions.
In Sagittarius:	produces expansiveness and love of adventure.
In Capricorn:	structures thought and action.
In Aquarius:	indicates humanistic goals.
In Pisces:	inspires mystical visions and mediums.

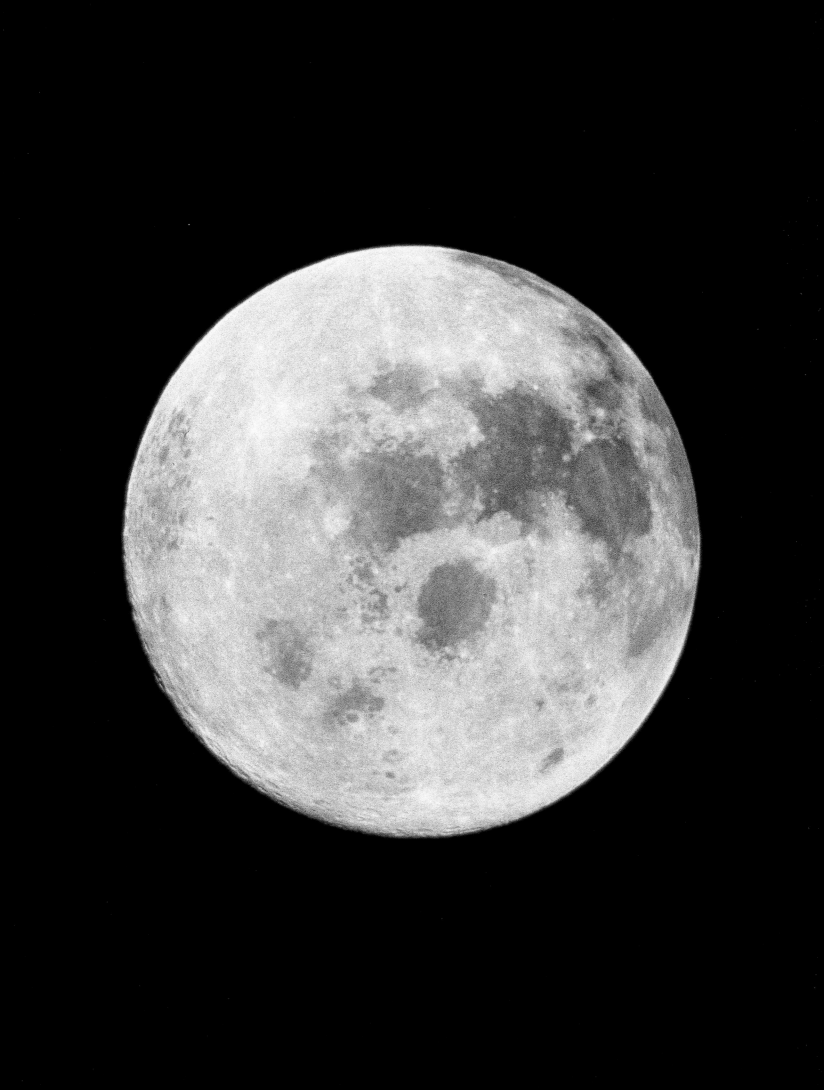

PHASES OF THE MOON

THE MYTH OF ETERNAL RETURN

THE MOON WAS THE FIRST INSTRUMENT USED TO MEASURE TIME. ETYMOLOGICALLY, THE LATIN WORD MENA, "MOON," PROVIDES the root "me" for the words "month," "measure," and so forth. The lunar cycle consists of four principal phases, which inspired the division into weeks. Each one lasts about seven days and represents a particular type of cosmic energy.

New moon   ●

First quarter (moon waxing)   ☽

Full moon   ○

Last quarter (moon waning)   ☾

From the new moon to the first quarter (from the first through the seventh day,) its thrust is at its height. This is the perfect time to start a new action or embark on a new project.

The first quarter of the full moon (from the eighth through the fourteenth day) is the first crisis: the limits of intervention are clearly apparent. There is a need to persist and force a way through without looking back.

The full moon to the last quarter (from the fifteenth through the twenty-first day) represents the first assessment. One can measure the result of an action begun in the new moon. It is also the best period for developing a project.

The last quarter of the new moon (from the twenty-second through the twenty-eighth day) is for the overall summary and projection. Three days before the new moon, consider the activities to be performed during the following cycle.

SOLI-LUNAR TYPES

The sun, as a *spirit*, impregnates the moon with its light. The nocturnal heavenly body symbolizes the capacity to adapt to the changes and challenges of life on Earth. This is why the phase of the moon at birth is important, which can be found in the ephemeris. Astrology has eight soli-lunar archetypes: the waxing hemicycle symbolizes constructive power, the waning hemicycle, propagation of new ideas.

New moon type (born at the time of the new moon or in the following 3½ days) : subjective, impulsive, and emotive character.

Waxing type (born 3½–7 days after the new moon) : fight between a reforming tendency and established structures.

First quarter type (born 7–10½ days after the new moon) : the subject seeks to establish frameworks for new structures.

Gibbous type (born in the 3½ days before the new moon) : emphasizes spiritual development.

Full moon type (born during the full moon or in the next 3½ days): a clear conscience makes fulfillment of the self possible.

Diffuser type (born 3½ days–7 days after the full moon) : propagator of new ideas.

Last quarter type (born 7–10½ days after the full moon) : tendency to put ideas before people.

Balsamic type (born in the last 3 days before the new moon): prophetic personality with a sense of "mission."

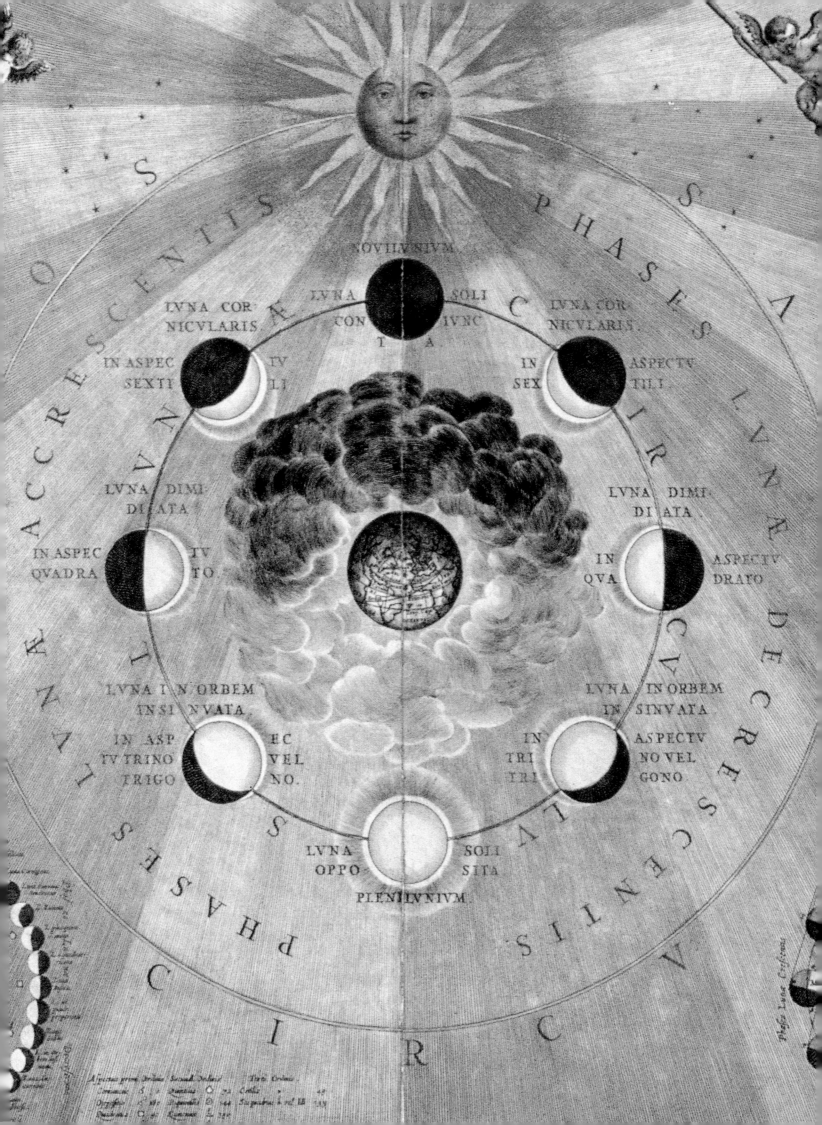

PHASES LVNÆ

NOVILVNIVM

LVNA COR-
NICVLARIS
LVNA SOLI
CON   IVNC
T   A
LVNA COR-
NICVLARIS

IN ASPEC   TV
SEXTI   LI
IN   ASPECTV
SEX   TILI

LVNA DIMI-
DIATA
LVNA DIMI-
DIATA

IN ASPEC   TV
QVADRA   TO
IN   ASPECTV
QVA   DRATO

LVNA IN ORBEM
INSINVATA
LVNA IN ORBEM
INSINVATA

IN ASP   EC
TV TRINO   VEL
TRIGO   NO
IN   ASPECTV
TRI   NOVEL
TRI   GONO

LVNA SOLI
OPPO   SITA
PLENILVNIVM

PHASES LVNÆ CIRCVLVS

MERCURY

MERCURY IS A TINY PLANET ONLY AS BIG AS THE MOON, WHICH FOLLOWS A COURSE INSIDE THE EARTH'S ORBIT. IT IS THE FASTEST moving planet and the nearest to the sun (about 36 million miles away), encircling the sun every 88 days. Its rotation on its own axis lasts 58 days, 15 hours and 38 minutes. In a chart, it is shown in the same sign as the sun or the next one to it. The images captured by space exploration vehicles show a contrasting, mountainous surface, pockmarked with craters.

In Greek mythology, Hermes led travelers and the spirits of the dead, and personified trickery. In Rome, he became Mercury, the god of merchants, theft and the lie (!), measurement and health. For the astrologer, the symbolism of Mercury today covers such varied fields as intelligence, communication, trade, travel, and physical fitness.

In alchemy, the ideogram of Mercury also served to designate quicksilver (mercury) as well as the "New Adam," an androgynous and ambiguous creature like an adolescent. Wednesday is Mercury's day of the week.

ELEMENT: Earth.

TIME OF LIFE: adolescence.

PRINCIPLE: communication, liaison, exchanges.

PSYCHOLOGY: nervous, intellectual, mocking, eloquent, expressive, immature.

OCCUPATIONS: interpreter, instructor, publisher, actor, secretary, chairperson.

SYMBOLS: brother, neighbor, colleague.

CHARACTERISTICS	POSITIVE	NEGATIVE
PERSONAL	Orderly, lover of detail, optimistic, easy-going.	Obsessiveness, irritability, instability.
SOCIAL	Curiosity, didactic nature, grace, speed, humor, charm, likeability.	Superficiality, dishonesty.
EMOTIONAL	Lightness, modernity, tolerance, fairness.	Cynicism, criticality, irresponsibility.

MERCURY WITHIN THE SIGNS

In Aries:	confers intuition, a sense of improvisation.
In Taurus:	confers practicality and a sense of reality.
In Gemini:	vivacity, mischievousness, and an aptitude for business.
In Cancer:	brings sensory and intuitive intelligence.
In Leo:	enlightens action by its nobility and lucidity.
In Virgo:	indicates a logical and organized mind.
In Libra:	indicates an aptitude for evaluation and comparison.
In Scorpio:	confers a penetrating and caustic mind.
In Sagittarius:	brings a sense of the universal and distant horizons.
In Capricorn:	confers a dispassionate viewpoint and a quest for the essential.
In Aquarius:	gives a progressive spirit and belief in reform.
In Pisces:	opens the mind to mediums and the ineffable.

VENUS

THIS IS THE STAR OF THE SHEPHERD, THE SEC-
OND PLANET FROM THE SUN AND THE
BRIGHTEST IN THE NIGHT SKY. IT IS SIMILAR
in size and density to the Earth, but turns very
slowly on its own axis, taking 243 earth-days to
do so. It appears to be hidden behind a dense
atmosphere which produces a greenhouse effect.
Venus never moves far from the sun (it is always
at a distance of about 67.5 million miles
away)—one or two signs at most in an individual chart—and it describes a five-petaled rose
around the Earth.

The peaks of Venus' volcanic surface have been
named after famous women, including Helen,
Sappho, Cleopatra, and even Marilyn Monroe.
We know how important Aphrodite/Venus was in
Greek and Roman mythology. She was the goddess of beauty and love, sensual pleasure and fertility. Her cult involved numerous rites and sacrifices. Venus has always represented femininity.

In alchemy, the ideogram of Venus also designates copper and female polarity. Friday is her day
of the week.

ELEMENT: Air.

TIME OF LIFE: the flower of youth.

PRINCIPLE: attraction, charm, likeability.

PSYCHOLOGY: romance, sensation and sensuality,
desire, celebration, seduction.

OCCUPATIONS: singing, dancing, the arts, beauty,
cosmetics, pleasure.

SYMBOLS: femininity, leisure, the arts, favors.

CHARACTERISTICS	POSITIVE	NEGATIVE
PERSONAL	Gentleness, amiability, generosity, emotionality, charm, prodigality.	Laziness, lethargy, irrealism.
SOCIAL	Likeability, adaptability, elegance, refinement, availability, coquetry.	Dependence, indecision, hypocrisy.
EMOTIONAL	Affection, attention, care of the home, punctuality, sensuality.	Possessiveness, sloth, lust, jealousy.

VENUS IN THE SIGNS

In Aries:	reinforces magnetism and predisposes to love at first sight.
In Taurus:	confers a practical spirit and sense of reality.
In Gemini:	brings lightness and a carefree spirit.
In Cancer:	emphasizes romanticism and love of domesticity.
In Leo:	indicates pride and a taste for display.
In Virgo:	characterizes reserve and modesty.
In Libra:	provides delicacy, coquettishness and ambivalence.
In Scorpio:	indicates an extreme, passionate and sensual nature.
In Sagittarius:	inspires rebelliousness and voyages of the spirit.
In Capricorn:	intellectualizes emotional life, adds frigidity.
In Aquarius:	idealizes sentiment, especially loving friendship.
In Pisces:	gives rise to multiple affections, inspires a taste for the unusual.

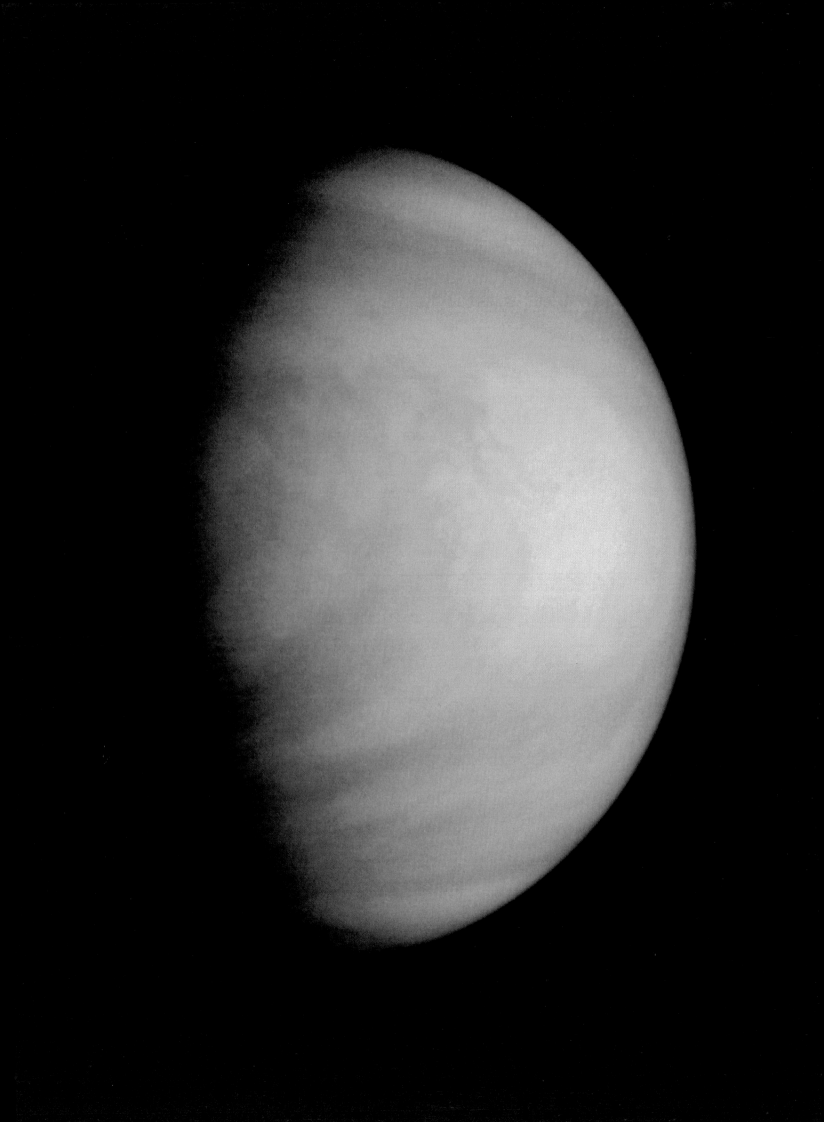

MARS

MARS IS THE FIRST OF THE SO-CALLED HIGHER PLANETS, WHOSE COURSE LIES OUTSIDE THE EARTH'S ORBIT. IN INDIVIDUAL CHARTS, THE position of Mars is not linked to that of the sun. Mars takes about two and a half years to cross the zodiac, and every fifteen years its orbit brings it quite close to us. The planet has been photographed by the "Mariner" satellites showing that it is generally orange in color, with a landscape pockmarked by craters. Although no life forms have been detected on the surface, the possibility of life underground has not been ruled out.

For the Romans, Mars was the god of war, father of the twin founders of Rome, Romulus and Remus. He ruled the spring and youth. His function was to protect the state, and he was thus combative, strong, brave. Mars has always represented virility *par excellence*.

The ideogram of Mars is also that of iron in alchemy. In fact, space exploration by the *Viking* probe has shown that Mars is particularly rich in iron, its third most common element. On Earth, iron is only the seventh most common. Mars day of the week is Tuesday.

ELEMENT: Fire.

TIME OF LIFE: maturity.

PRINCIPLE: confrontation.

PSYCHOLOGY: anger, extroversion, hostility.

OCCUPATIONS: police, army, sports.

SYMBOLS: passion, combat, war, fire, accidents, trials, burning.

CHARACTERISTICS	POSITIVE	NEGATIVE
PERSONAL	Bravura, loyalty, decisiveness, warmth.	Aggression, brutality, cruelty, violence.
SOCIAL	A desire for a challenge, courage, enthusiasm, aptitude for leadership, team spirit.	Temerity, impulsiveness, rudeness, anger.
EMOTIONAL	Passion, strong emotions, non-conformist.	Quarrelsome, ironic, sadistic.

MARS IN THE SIGNS

In Aries:	inclined to violent action, taking an uncompromising position.
In Taurus:	emphasizes instinctive excesses.
In Gemini:	gives a taste for fierce debates.
In Cancer:	aggression is directed at the family or institutions.
In Leo:	intensifies the appetite for conquest.
In Virgo:	produces lucidity and discipline, inspires elegant strategies.
In Libra:	expresses diplomacy and the search for compromise.
In Scorpio:	emphasizes refinement and determination.
In Sagittarius:	confers brilliance and humanity to actions.
In Capricorn:	produces a character of tempered steel, tenacious and political.
In Aquarius:	indicates adventurous goals and fraternal objectives.
In Pisces:	indicates spiritual and religious goals.

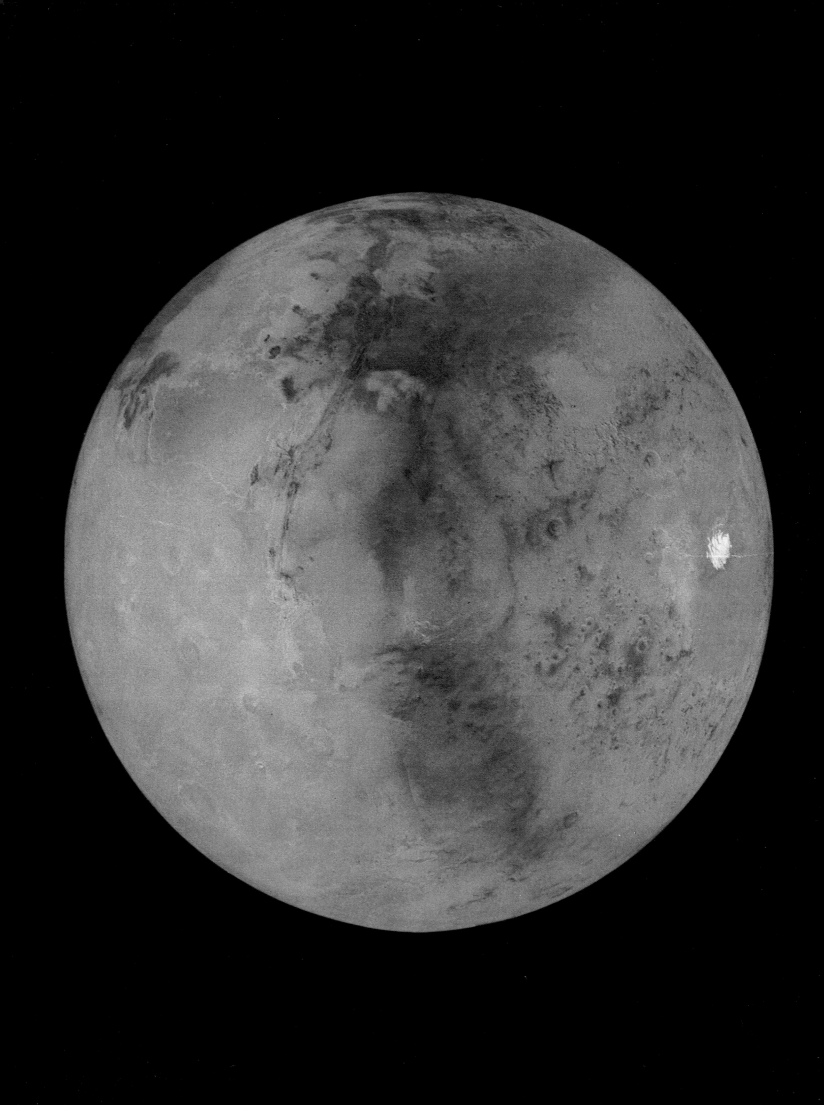

JUPITER

$$\text{4}$$

JUPITER IS THE LARGEST PLANET IN THE SOLAR SYSTEM AND FIFTH FROM THE SUN. IT HAS AT LEAST SIXTEEN SATELLITES OF ITS OWN AND takes only nine hours to rotate on its own axis, but twelve years to circle around the zodiac.

For the Ancients, Jupiter represented a patriarchal divinity, generous and majestic. The name derives from *Zeus* (god) and *pater* (father.) Zeus was very taken with affairs of the heart. Although married to the goddess Hera, he had many extramarital affairs. His host of illegitimate children included Athena, who sprang from his thigh, then the Destinies, who governed the lives of humans. With the nymph Mnemosyne (Memory), he conceived the nine Muses: Calliope, protectress of epic poetry and eloquence; Clio, patroness of history; Erato, who presided over erotic poetry and weddings; Euterpe, who ruled celebrations; Melpomene, patroness of singing and harmony, and then tragedy; Polymnia, who was said to preside over anthems, mime, and lyrical poetry; Terpsichore, responsible for dance; Thalia, patroness of comedy and light verse; and Urania, patroness of astronomy. For the Romans, Jupiter represented the main divinity in the pantheon, governor of light and the elements: thunder, lightning and the climate. He ensured that the social hierarchy was maintained, presided over international relations and protocol, dispensed good and evil.

His ideogram is also used to designate tin, and his day of the week is Thursday.

ELEMENT: Air.

TIME OF LIFE: maturity.

PRINCIPLE: order, cohesion, organization.

PSYCHOLOGY: extroversion, expansion, honor, opulence, prestige.

OCCUPATIONS: judge, lawyer, actor, banker.

SYMBOLS: dignitaries and VIPs.

CHARACTERISTICS	POSITIVE	NEGATIVE
PERSONAL	Optimism, extroversion, joviality, generosity charisma, largesse.	Lack of discernment, practical joking.
SOCIAL	Gift for languages, the law, politics, diplomacy, taste for representation.	Pride, excess, delusions of grandeur, prodigality.
EMOTIONAL	Likeability, hospitality, sense of comfort, availability, warmth.	Indolence, opportunism, authoritarianism.

JUPITER IN THE SIGNS

In Aries:	contributes reactivity, power and expertise.
In Taurus:	reinforces the sanguine, jovial, and sensual temperament.
In Gemini:	gives a gift for diplomacy and eloquence.
In Cancer :	confers domestic qualities and a sense of family.
In Leo:	emphasizes the majestic character, full of panache.
In Virgo:	brings a sense of proportion and convention.
In Libra:	gives qualities of conciliation and negotiation.
In Scorpio:	emphasizes magnetism and the creative instinct.
In Sagittarius:	confers spirit, generosity and a taste for adventure.
In Capricorn:	emphasizes social ambition and political qualities.
In Aquarius:	produces a warm, vibrant, and caring nature.
In Pisces:	reinforces availability, hospitality and charisma.

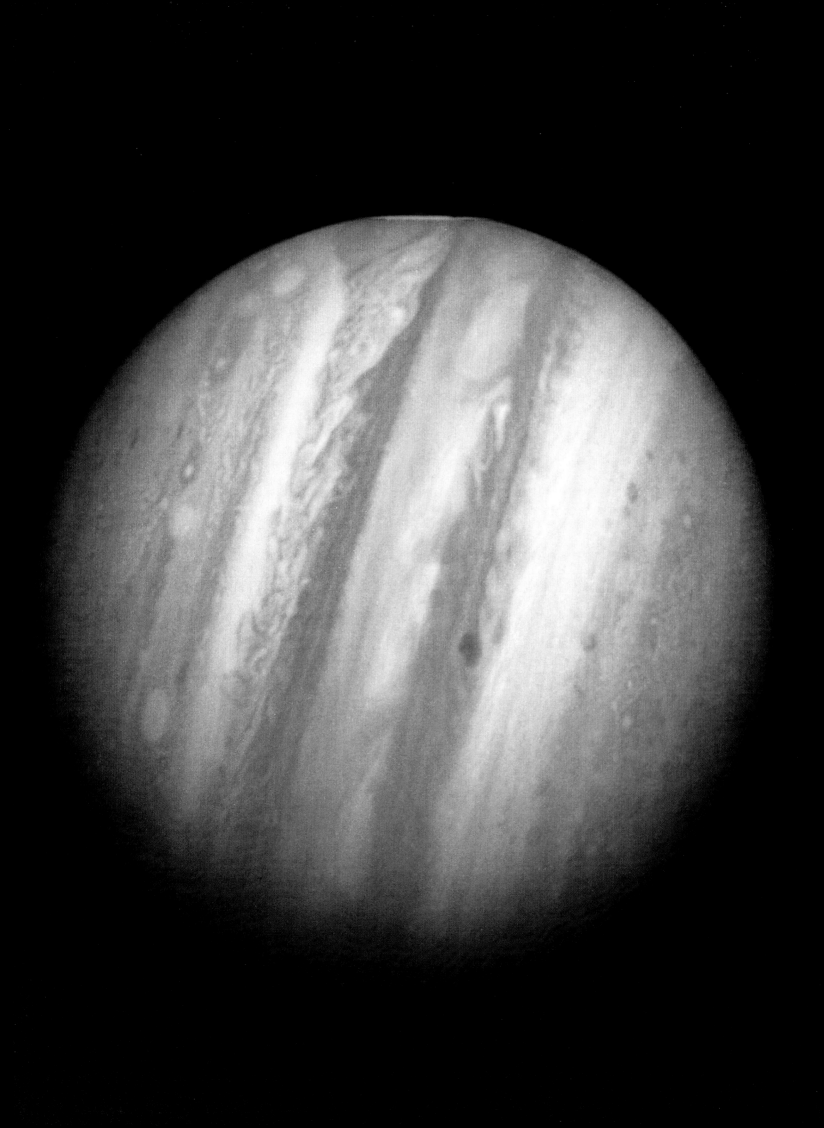

SATURN

SATURN IS A DISTANT PLANET, SIXTH IN THE ORDER OF DISTANCE FROM THE SUN (900 MILLION MILES AWAY). IT IS A LARGE PLANET, more than nine times the diameter of Earth. When studied through a telescope, Saturn is a grayish-yellow color but its main feature is the nine concentric rings around it, which are the debris from disintegrated satellites. *Voyager* probes have discovered twenty-three Saturnine satellites, the largest of which is Titan. It takes Saturn 29 years and 167 days to go once around the sun. This length of time has an effect on human life: passages of Saturn mark periods of reflection and personal doubt. Astrology is interested in changes in the signs of Saturn, which happen about every two and a half years and affect psychological growth.

In mythology, represented by a sickle and a hook, Saturn was the god of sowing (*satus*) and cultivation of the vine. Saturn, the son of Uranus—whom he punished—became supreme ruler of the Earth. The legends about him show him as having a cruel and jealous temperament. Saturn's myth is linked to restriction and, through identification with Cronos, with time, its limits, and its inevitable passing.

Saturn's ideogram is also used in alchemy to designate lead. His day is Saturday.

ELEMENT: Earth.

TIME OF LIFE: old age (return to the Earth).

PRINCIPLES: conservation, concentration, abstraction.

PSYCHOLOGY: detachment, asceticism, spirituality.

OCCUPATIONS: historian, scientist, researcher.

SYMBOLS: old people, sages.

CHARACTERISTICS	POSITIVE	NEGATIVE
PERSONAL	Prudence, practicality, economy, patience, endurance, stability.	Suspicion, malevolence, egotism, rigidity, cruelty.
SOCIAL	Discipline, sense of responsibility, solidity, reason, scientific mind.	Distance, frigidity, bitterness, sadness, indifference.
EMOTIONAL	Spirituality, comprehension, empathy.	Anxiety, melancholy, solitude, frustration.

SATURN IN THE SIGNS

In Aries:	brings daring and expertise to creation.
In Taurus:	emphasizes endurance and perseverance of character.
In Gemini:	structures and conceptualizes thought.
In Cancer:	inclines to solitude and depression.
In Leo:	confers magnificent isolation, and even renunciation.
In Virgo:	accentuates self-control and self-discipline.
In Libra:	confirms spirituality and detachment.
In Scorpio:	exacerbates tendencies toward inhibition and self-control.
In Sagittarius:	affirms spiritual and philosophical aspirations.
In Capricorn:	increases ability to concentrate and thoroughness.
In Aquarius:	provides spiritual and humanist detachment.
In Pisces:	symbolizes the solitude of the spirit and a taste for sacrifice.

URANUS

URANUS, THE SEVENTH PLANET, IS A GIANT WHOSE DIAMETER IS MORE THAN FOUR TIMES THAT OF THE EARTH AND 1.73 BILLION MILES from the sun. It was discovered only recently by William Herschel in 1781. Uranus, which has nine rings and some fifteen moons, consists of condensed gases. The cold observed in its clouds may well trap a quantity of heat on the surface. Its retrograde motion on its own axis lasts for only about seventeen hours, so the Uranian day is seven hours shorter than our own. Its sidereal revolution lasts eighty-eight years. As with all the trans-Saturnine planets (Uranus, Neptune, and Pluto), its astrological influence has grown with time.

Changes in the sign of Uranus occur roughly every seven years and mark a collective transformation in the human race. According to tradition, the discovery of Uranus coincides with the American and French Revolutions. The principle of change—rupture and overthrow—thus result. Its connection to modern science (aeronautics, architecture, the conquest of space) are also linked to this sociological turning point and the industrial revolution.

As the master of Aquarius, Uranus will symbolically reign over the cosmic age that we are about to enter.

ELEMENT: Fire.

PRINCIPLE S: intensity, individualism.

PSYCHOLOGY: challenge, modernity, non-conformity.

SYMBOLS: rockets, lasers.

CHARACTERISTICS	POSITIVE	NEGATIVE
PERSONAL	Independence, action, inventiveness, originality, genius.	Eccentricity, rebelliousness, perversity, oddness.
SOCIAL	Inquiring mind, ingenuity, faith, prowess, idealism.	Frenzy, delusions, paranoia.
EMOTIONAL	Non-conformity, authority, empathy.	Instability, capriciousness, unrealistic attitudes.

URANUS IN THE SIGNS

In Aries:	indicates a reforming and daring spirit.
In Taurus:	evidence of constancy in progressive research.
In Gemini:	disciplines intellectual values.
In Cancer :	permits an extended concept of the family.
In Leo:	contributes passion and extravagance.
In Virgo:	seeks self-denial and discipline.
In Libra:	humanizes the Uranian adventure.
In Scorpio:	brings excess in passion.
In Sagittarius:	directs the Uranian quest toward spiritual adventure.
In Capricorn:	reinforces individual authority.
In Aquarius:	emphasizes scientific abilities.
In Pisces:	introduces thoroughness and the sense of collectivity.

NEPTUNE

NEPTUNE WAS DISCOVERED BY THE GERMAN ASTRONOMER GALLE IN 1846 BASED ON THE FINDINGS OF THE BRITISH ASTRONOMER Adams and the Frenchman Le Verrier. It is the eighth planet in order of distance from the sun. Although four times the size of the Earth, Neptune's rotation on its axis takes only eighteen hours. Its revolution around the sun, which takes 164 years and 280 days, represents the period between two successive passages of Neptune through the same point of the zodiac. Therefore, Neptune does not transit a natal chart during a human lifetime. The planet stays in each sign for about fourteen years, but its influence increases through currents of collective thought.

As with Uranus, the discovery of Neptune corresponds to an historic date. In 1848, there was a socialist revolution in France followed by uprisings elsewhere in Europe, an event known collectively as "the people's spring." The symbolism of the planet is attached to this phenomenon, in the form of universalist values, sensitivity, empathy, and compassion for the dispossessed, as well as imagination and inspiration. The name of the planet is linked, of course, to Neptune-Poseidon, god of the Oceans, and one of the three masters of the Universe.

ELEMENT: Water.
PRINCIPLE: permeability, participation, communion.
PSYCHOLOGY: plasticity, receptivity, availability.
SYMBOLS: collectivism, mysticism.

CHARACTERISTICS	POSITIVE	NEGATIVE
PERSONAL	Sensitivity, humanity, plasticity, intuition.	Suggestibility, gullibility, a taste for artificial delights.
SOCIAL	Artistic gifts, altruism, group participation, imagination.	Irrationality, confusion, contemplation, amorality, various anxieties.
EMOTIONAL	Gentleness, poetry, romanticism, inventiveness, availability.	Indecision, lies, ambivalence.

NEPTUNE IN THE SIGNS

In Aries:	provides a desire for adventure, tinged with utopianism.
In Taurus:	accentuates sensuality, escapism, and mysticism.
In Gemini:	cerebralizes emotive tendencies.
In Cancer:	emphasizes sensitivity and maternal qualities.
In Leo:	confers a flamboyant and baroque imagination.
In Virgo:	defines and limits the boundaries of imagination.
In Libra:	develops esthetic and spiritual tendencies.
In Scorpio:	emphasizes aspirations to mysticism and the occult.
In Sagittarius:	reinforces imaginative and humanitarian qualities.
In Capricorn:	restrains and confines emotional availability.
In Aquarius:	contributes humanity and mysticism.
In Pisces:	accentuates sensitivity and spirituality.

PLUTO

OF ALL THE KNOWN PLANETS, PLUTO IS THE FURTHEST FROM THE SUN. ITS DIAMETER IS ONE FOURTH THAT OF THE EARTH, AND ITS mass five times less. Pluto takes six days, nine hours to rotate on its own axis; its sidereal revolution takes 248 years and 57 days. It was discovered in 1930 by the American astronomer, Clyde William Tombaugh, but the work of Percival Lowell and Edward Pickering concerning the irregularities of Neptune indicated its existence as early as 1915 (Pluto may be a former satellite of Neptune).

These observations were made during a particularly troublesome period in history involving the Russian Revolution of 1917, the Wall Street Crash of 1929 and the subsequent Depression, and the rise of Fascism in Europe. Simultaneously, the success of psychoanalysis led to the flourishing of various schools of psychology. In 1930, Freud published *Civilization and its Discontents*.

The symbolism of Pluto is associated with these events. For the astrologer, the mythical master of the nether regions governs the values linked with the unconscious. However, the legend of the "bestower of wealth" god (a plutocracy is government by the wealthy) translates into a fertile and beneficial influence.

PRINCIPLE: death and renaissance.
PSYCHOLOGY: unconscious depths.
SYMBOLS: hidden wealth.

CHARACTERISTICS	POSITIVE	NEGATIVE
PERSONAL	Richness and depth, higher intelligence, genius.	Morbid imagination, delirium, neurosis.
SOCIAL	Analytical mind, curiosity, metaphysics, ambition, love of risk and challenge.	Destruction, obsessions, self-destruction.
EMOTIONAL	Universal conscience, higher sensitivity.	Sadism, perversion, taste for the forbidden.

PLUTO IN THE SIGNS

In Aries: exacerbates aggression.
In Taurus: intensifies passion.
In Gemini: fertilizes mental research.
In Cancer: indicates subversion and psychological crises.
In Leo: affirms its power with panache.
In Virgo: assigns limits to aggression.
In Libra: indicates a liberal philosophy.
In Scorpio: gives priority to sexuality.
In Sagittarius: inspires an expanded vision of existence.
In Capricorn: creates axes of political organization.
In Aquarius: opens the mind to the transpersonal and social.
In Pisces: indicate a profound mysticism.

THE PLANETARY CYCLES

THE SEVEN AGES OF MAN

THE ANCIENTS OBSERVED SIMILARITIES BE-TWEEN THE RHYTHMS OF THE UNIVERSE AND THE PHASES OF HUMAN LIFE AND ELABORATED a theory of the ages of man, associating a planet with each stage of human life. According to them, the moon governed humans from birth to the age of four, then Mercury took over until the age of fourteen. Venus arrived in adolescence, from 15 through 22, then came the sun, from 23 to 41 years of age. The time of conflict, from 42 through 46 years of age belonged to Mars, before Jupiter reviewed the situation between 57 and 68 years. Saturn finally reigned over old age. This is an interesting theory but one which has fallen into disuse since modern astrologers prefer the theory of cycles.

A *cycle* is the time taken by a planet to complete a revolution. The lunar cycle (twenty-eight days) influences female physiology. Jupiter's cycle lasts twelve years—making one year per sign. Each phase affects social life. For instance, when Jupiter reaches Aries, it galvanizes the Fire signs. The following year, when it is in Taurus, it will affect the Earth signs.

The cycle of Saturn lasts for twenty-nine and a half years and its main stages mark the awareness of passing time: loss of innocence, entry into adulthood, lucidity, maturity, old age.

Uranus' cycle lasts eighty-four years, about as long as a human lifetime. Uranus is the planet of individual influence and its cycle presents as many changes as those of an individual personality.

These cycles consist of several phases which punctuate existence and symbolize key moments in spiritual development.

At *seven years of age* there is an awakening of the personality. The child becomes aware of his or her individuality and instinctively tries to measure it against that of others. Seven is the age of the *first square of Saturn*.

The *twelfth* birthday symbolizes *Jupiter's return to the natal position*. There is generally a creative awakening of the child as well as his or her birth on the social level.

Puberty, around the age of *fifteen*, marks a disruptive and rebellious phase, corresponding in the individual chart to the *opposition of Saturn*.

Subsequently, the individual comes of age at *twenty-one*, the age of the *second square of Saturn*. This is an important milestone, that of emancipation and civic responsibility.

Twenty-four marks Jupiter's second return, an exciting time when desire for success and creating a family and home are the focus.

The first crisis of adulthood occurs at around the age of *twenty nine*, with the *first return of Saturn to the natal position*. In the astral chart, the planet has now performed a complete cycle. As with all the Saturnine phases, this one requires an effort at thoroughness, a return to self, and personal definition—with the accompanying rejection and rupture. *Thirty-six*, with the *square*

of Saturn and a *return of Jupiter,* is an age for perfecting what has gone before in order to make new investments in life. Three planes are simultaneously in operation. There is social identity, personal experience and spiritual questioning. It is a time of ambiguity in which Jovian enthusiasm is in conflict with the often bitter lucidity of Saturn.

With the *double opposition of Uranus and Jupiter,* and the *first square of Neptune, the age of forty-two* often represents a sensitive milestone, that of new beginnings and coming to terms with the consequences of youth—and lost illusions!

The *forty-eighth birthday* celebrates the prime of life. After four *Jovian cycles,* the social position is reinforced and its rewards are reaped.

At *fifty-six,* the *trine of Uranus* is an age of great satisfaction. There are new responsibilities, among them teaching and learning, which make it possible to look back on the road traversed.

Three planets can be found in *pole position* when the person reaches the age of *fifty-nine/sixty. The return of Saturn, return of Jupiter* and *square of Pluto,* are among the factors which determine a profound desire for the truth. Philosophical reflection and the start of wisdom do not impair Jovian expansion.

The *seventy-second birthday* is a celebration of patriarchy or matriarchy, a glorious *return of Jupiter* to its natal position—for the sixth time.

At *eighty-four,* there is the cosmic privilege of experiencing the *return of Uranus* to its natal position, resulting in initiation into his or her immortality and new creative or spiritual directions.

The Seven Ages of the Life of a Woman, *Hans Baldung Grien. Oil on wood, 1544.*

ASTROLOGICAL HOUSES

THE TERRESTRIAL HOURS

THE ASTROLOGICAL HOUSES SYMBOLIZE THE HOURS OF THE DAY. THERE ARE TWELVE HOUSES OR SECTORS, JUST AS THERE ARE twelve signs, each with its own particular significance. Each house represents a two-hour segment of time. The *Ascendant* or First House is a sign which rises in the eastern horizon of the chart, at about 6:00 A.M. The *Midheaven* marks noon, the *Descendant* 6:00 P.M. and the *Imum Coeli (IC)*, or lowest point of the sky, midnight. *Domification*, or calculation of the Houses, is an operation involving spherical trigonometry, which consists of establishing the positions of the angular Houses, and then deducting the positions of the intermediate Houses from it. There are several tables of Houses calculated for various latitudes, including those of Placidus (named for Placidus de Tito, a seventeenth-century Italian astronomer and astrologer), that are most commonly used. Others are those of Regiomontanus, Campanus, and Koch. These tables agree on the degrees of the Ascendant and Midheaven, but differ with respect to the intermediate Houses, thus making little difference to the interpretation of the chart.

A Greco-Egyptian tradition has given each of the twelve Houses a symbolism related to images from daily life. These images have changed and developed through the ages.

THE FIRST HOUSE (or Ascendant):
The world of self: one's personal concept and self-image. The subject as he sees himself or herself and the image that he or she projects.

THE SECOND HOUSE:
Material wealth and finances: assets, possessions, and risks of existence linked to wealth.

THE THIRD HOUSE:
Communication, immediate contacts (siblings, neighbors): correspondence (letters, phone calls, faxes, email); short trips; short pieces of writing (poems, songs); learning, intellectual pursuits.

THE FOURTH HOUSE (or Imum Coeli [IC]):
Home, family (parents, ancestors): origins, family home; one's own home and those with whom the subject shares it.

THE FIFTH HOUSE:
The universe of creation: production of the mind. *Recreation:* games and amusements. Gambling and romance. *Procreation:* children.

THE SIXTH HOUSE:
Daily life: work and health (minor illnesses); routine (constraints, workload, insurance, etc.); subordinates, servants, and pets.

THE SEVENTH HOUSE (or Descendant):
Marriage and official love life (union, divorce): joint ventures, social activity (associations, contracts, law suits).

THE EIGHTH HOUSE:
Sexuality and eroticism (Eros): transformation and regeneration. *Mental breakdowns, death,*

destruction (Thanatos). ***Rebirth:*** inheritance, legacies, and other people's money in general.

THE NINTH HOUSE:

Religion, philosophy, travel to distant places: education, mystical revelations, vocation.

THE TENTH HOUSE (or Midheaven):

Social life, occupation, career: social position, reputation, accomplishments.

THE ELEVENTH HOUSE:

Chosen affinities and friendships: group activities and charitable works. ***Major projects*** (travel, starting a family, etc.).

THE TWELFTH HOUSE:

The soul and its peregrinations: Karma and proofs of existence. Spiritual life.

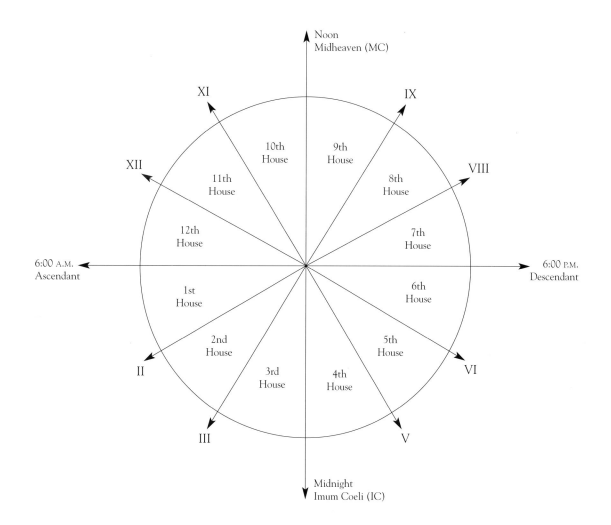

KARMA

___

THE THEORY OF PREVIOUS LIVES

BELIEF IN REINCARNATION CONSTITUTES ONE OF THE BASIC BELIEFS OF BUDDHISM. THE MINGLING OF EAST AND WEST AT THE END OF the old century and beginning of the new makes this a timely issue, since the West has begun to embrace this philosophy. The theory of previous lives makes it possible to imagine that the main events in our life—relationships, meetings, disappointments, successes, and good luck—are all related to events in our past lives. The word *karma*, borrowed from Buddhism, represents the baggage we have inherited from our past lives. This is the sum of past thoughts, words and deeds, embedded in our unconscious memories. By virtue of the law of action and reaction, we reap what we have sown. Memory is reactivated with current experiences. We are constantly creating a new *karma* ("deed" in Sanskrit) through our thoughts and deeds, based on our ancient roots. In other words, we re-evaluate the past through our present attitude. That is why it is a delicate matter to talk of destiny. We create our own destiny day after day, by tracing new routes on the basis of pre-existing axes. One of our aims in life is to right wrongs committed in our past lives to receive gratification.

How can one know one's karma? Astrology offers a key through special points known as *Lunar Nodes*. An ancient tradition inherited from India links two energies, that of karma and our past incarnations with that of our future. The position of the Lunar Nodes depends on one's date of birth. They remain in each sign for about eighteen months (*see table on page 87.*)

THE NORTHERN LUNAR NODE IN THE SIGNS

In Aries: present existence is underpinned by an imperative need for action and desire to go beyond the limits, social or geographical. In reaction to a series of slothful lives, you will never stop toiling.

In Taurus: today, the soul aspires to rest and seeks to be spared from unnecessary shocks. You are attracted by mystery but can only take it in small doses, because you are disconcerted by irrationality. Your pugnacity of yesterday will be concentrated mainly on material goals.

In Gemini: the experience of previous lives offers you an irresistible challenge. Your intellectual curiosity is a source of joy and stimulation. Your karma will thus place you in a position of privilege, but it would be a mistake to abuse it. Career-related disappointments and problems with relationships will teach you the relative value of success.

In Cancer : building a nest, sheltered from external aggression, and snuggling into it is your main goal. No question of traveling through the world on your own, you need a large entourage and a stable base camp. You perpetuate family traditions, while jealously clinging to your moral values.

In Leo: you retain your caring and generous nature from your glorious past incarnations. You have the qualities of a leader: charisma, authority and an innate nobility. The idealism which is innate in you causes you to work for the underprivileged. The need to improve society causes you to act and take sides. You retain your vocation for humanitarian struggles.

Facing page: The Astrologers (detail), Tarikh-i-Khandan-i-Timuriyah. Undated.
Following page: astrological manuscript written on palm-leaf. India, 17th century.

In Virgo: you try to learn your lesson from your karmic experiences by first relying on material things. Even if you have retained the benefits of the past in the form of a tendency to consult mediums and a taste for irrationality, you tend to devote most of your current life to reality. You choose to place your gifts in the service of scientific knowledge.

In Libra: in this incarnation you will adopt associative measures. Your inexhaustible energy will be all the more appreciated if it is tamed and made more flexible. Work is the key word. Work on yourself at first, in harmony with others. You also seek success and material comforts, without, however, becoming subservient to this objective.

In Scorpio: safety and conformity are the two values which have guided your choices in a previous existence, but they lose any relevance in this one. On the contrary, your current life contains a high degree of instability which will cause you to question it constantly—with positive results.

In Sagittarius: as a reaction to the past, in your current existence, you seek less to conform to the values imposed by others than to comply with your own values. You define your own code quite early on, and it is this personal code which counts the most in your eyes.

In Capricorn: you will develop an irrepressible need to express yourself through your occupation. You may even become brilliantly successful at it. Today, unlike yesterday, it is in the outside world, and not in the family, that you will put down roots. Work and career will be the backdrop for your most important feelings.

In Aquarius: from a sequence of past lives you will retain prestige and material wealth. You will quickly rise to a position of influence without making any special effort. Within your chosen profession, you will develop important responsibilities and gain the position of mediator.

In Pisces: your life will be mainly one of caring. Material comfort will mean less to you than a sense of action. You will retain from a sequence of previous lives a predisposition to philosophize and mediate. Use these gifts to purify your thoughts and avoid any hint of censure.

TABLE OF NORTHERN LUNAR NODES (♌)

Date of birth	Lunar node
From 15.08.1919 at 4:00 A.M. to 07.02.1921 at 1:00 P.M.	SCORPIO
From 07.02.1921 at 1:00 P.M. to 23.08.1922 at 2:00 P.M.	LIBRA
From 23.08.1922 at 2:00 P.M. to 22.04.1924 at 6:00 P.M.	VIRGO
From 22.04.1924 at 6:00 P.M. to 26.10.1925 at 9:00 P.M.	LEO
From 26.10.1925 at 9:00 P.M. to 16.04.1927 at 1:00A.M.	CANCER
From 16.04.1927 at 1:00 A.M. to 28.12.1928 at 3:00 P.M.	GEMINI
From 28.12.1928 at 3:00 P.M. to 07.07.1930 at 5:00 A.M.	TAURUS
From 07.07.1930 at 5:00 A.M. to 28.12.1931 at 9:00 P.M.	ARIES
From 28.12.1931 at 9:00 P.M. to 24.06.1933 at 7:00 A.M.	PISCES
From 24.06.1933 at 7:00 A.M. to 08.03.1935 at 10:00 A.M.	AQUARIUS
From 08.03.1935 at 10:00 A.M. to 14.09.1936 at 10:00 P.M.	CAPRICORN
From 14.09.1936 at 10:00 P.M. to 03.03.1938 at 4:00 A.M.	SAGITTARIUS
From 03.03.1938 at 4:00 A.M. to 11.09.1939 at 5:00 P.M.	SCORPIO
From 11.09.1939 at 5:00 P.M. to 24.05.1941 at 3:00 P.M.	LIBRA
From 24.05.1941 at 3:00 P.M. to 21.11.1942 at 10:00 P.M.	VIRGO
From 21.11.1942 at 10:00 P.M. to 11.05.1944 at 4:00 P.M.	LEO
From 11.05.1944 at 4:00 P.M. to 03.12.1945 at 9:00 A.M.	CANCER
From 03.12.1945 at 9:00 A.M. to 02.08.1947 at 4:00 A.M.	GEMINI
From 02.08.1947 at 4:00 A.M. to 26.01.1949 at noon	TAURUS
From 26.01.1949 at noon to 26.07.1950 at 2:00 A.M.	ARIES
From 26.07.1950 at 2:00 A.M. to 28.03.1952 at 11:00 P.M.	PISCES
From 28.03.1952 at 11:00 P.M. to 09.10.1953 at 9:00 A.M.	AQUARIUS
From 09.10.1953 at 9:00A.M. to 02.04.1955 at 4:00 A.M.	CAPRICORN
From 02.04.1955 at 4:00 A.M. to 04.10.1956 at 5:00 A.M.	SAGITTARIUS
From 04.10.1956 at 5:00 A.M. to 16.01.1958 at 4:00 P.M.	SCORPIO
From 16.01.1958 at 4:00 P.M. to 15.12.1959 at 4:00 A.M.	LIBRA
From 15.12.1959 at 4:00 A.M. to 10.06.1961 at 10:00 A.M.	VIRGO

Date of birth	Lunar node
From 10.06.1961 at 10:00 A.M. to 23.12.1962 at 8:00 P.M.	LEO
From 23.12.1962 at 8:00 P.M. to 25.08.1964 at 5:00 A.M.	CANCER
From 25.08.1964 at 5:00 A.M. to 19.02.1966 at 8:00 P.M.	GEMINI
From 19.02.1966 at 8:00 P.M. to 19.08.1967 at 4:00 P.M.	TAURUS
From 19.08.1967 at 4:00 P.M. to 19.04.1969 at 8:00 P.M.	ARIES
From 19.04.1969 at 8:00 P.M. to 02.11.1970 at 7:00 A.M.	PISCES
From 02.11.1970 at 7:00 A.M. to 27.04.1972 at 1:00 P.M.	AQUARIUS
From 27.04.1972 at 1:00 P.M. to 27.10.1973 at noon	CAPRICORN
From 27.10.1973 at noon to 09.07.1975 at 9:00 P.M.	SAGITTARIUS
From 09.07.1975 at 9:00 P.M. to 07.01.1977 at 2:00 A.M.	SCORPIO
From 07.01.1977 at 2:00 A.M. to 05.07.1978 at 2:00 P.M.	LIBRA
From 05.07.1978 at 2:00 P.M. to 12.01.1980 at 1:00 P.M.	VIRGO
From 12.01.1980 at 1:00 P.M. to 24.09.1981 at 5:00 A.M.	LEO
From 24.09.1981 at 5:00 A.M. to 16.03.1983 at 8:00 A.M.	CANCER
From 16.03.1983 at 8:00 A.M. to 11.09.1984 at 8:00 A.M.	GEMINI
From 11.09.1984 at 8:00 A.M. to 06.04.1986 at 8:00 A.M.	TAURUS
From 06.04.1986 at 8:00 A.M. to 02.12.1987 at 5:00 A.M.	ARIES
From 02.12.1987 at 5:00 A.M. to 22.05.1989 at 5:00 P.M.	PISCES
From 22.05.1989 at 5:00 P.M. to 18.11.1990 at 3:00 P.M.	AQUARIUS
From 18.11.1990 at 3:00 P.M. to 01.08.1992 at 8:00 P.M.	CAPRICORN
From 01.08.1992 at 8:00 P.M. to 01.02.1994 at 6:00 A.M.	SAGITTARIUS
From 01.02.1994 at 6:00 A.M. to 01.08.1995 at 4:00 P.M.	SCORPIO
From 01.08.1995 at 4:00 P.M. to 26.01.1997 at 4:00 P.M.	LIBRA
From 26.01.1997 at 4:00 P.M. to 21.10.1998 at 4:00 A.M.	VIRGO
From 21.10.1998 at 4:00 A.M. to 10.04.2000 at 4:00 P.M.	LEO
From 10.04.2000 at 4:00 P.M. to 14.10.2001 at 4:00 A.M.	CANCER
From 14.10.2001 at 4:00 A.M. to 15.04.2003 at 5:00 A.M.	GEMINI

THE BLACK MOON

IN AN INDIVIDUAL HOROSCOPE, THE BLACK MOON DESIGNATES THE POINT EXACTLY OPPOSITE THE MOON. EACH STAGE OF THE lunar orbit thus has its virtually symmetrical counterpoint because its second home remains empty by definition.

The Black moon symbolizes that which is inaccessible, a perfection that it is impossible to attain in the course of a human life. This quest for the Holy Grail, which links mortals to the divinity, takes on a different appearance from one individual to the next.

The poet and astrologer Jean Carteret, when writing about "the sacrificial knife," associated it with the poem by Pierre Jean Jouve *Lady with a Unicorn*: "I die of thirst beside the fountain . . . ."

The unicorn, that fabulous animal, in its whiteness and with its single horn, symbolizes sexuality transcended. The myth of Lilith, the black counterpart of the primordial Eve and instigator or illegitimate love, paints this universe in a cruel light.

The symbolism of the Black moon thus appears to be among the most tormented. Its interpretation is a bone of contention among astrologers. Some schools do not take it into account at all, while others make excessive use of it. In fact, the Black moon does not have the same resonance in all cases. Generally, it is of particular importance in the chart of an artist or a philosopher—whenever the concept of renunciation or sublimation arises in the mind of the subject. Through its very symbolism, it remains more of a question than an answer in the study of a personality.

THE BLACK MOON IN THE HOUSES

First House: turns its back on stereotypes in order to affirm an individual Self.

Second House: refuses possessions—or suggests an ecological battle.

Third House: expresses research of language.

Fourth House: often accompanies atypical family relationships.

Fifth House: indicates a need at the creative and emotional level.

Sixth House: rejects habit in order to serve a cause or a love.

Seventh House: tries to avoid marriage and social rules.

Eighth House: tends to transcend the idea of death.

Ninth House: imposes the need for a personal moral code.

Tenth House: aims at distinction through originality.

Eleventh House: elevates thought and confers a high opinion of friendship.

Twelfth House: imposes a rigorous ethic, often accompanied by moral suffering.

Lady with a Unicorn. *Tapestry, late 15th century.*

ECLIPSES

BELIEFS AND HISTORY

THE ECLIPSE IS ONE OF THE MOST EXTRAORDINARY COSMIC PHENOMENA HUMANS CAN WITNESS. EVERY YEAR, IT AFFECTS BOTH THE light-givers, the sun and the moon, but is not visible everywhere on Earth. Eclipses have been recorded since the dawn of history and are associated with magic and prophesy. They are mentioned several times in the Bible. For Babylonians living in the sixth century B.C., they were a divine warning and required ritual sacrifices. Although the Babylonians were adept at predicting when an eclipse would occur, they were not able to say where it would be visible.

On a mythological level, the eclipse first inspired legends involving animals. The Chinese believed that a fabulous dragon arose and devoured the light of day; the Egyptians cursed the serpent Apophis, enemy of Ra, the Sun-God. In Paraguay and Argentina, the jaguar was blamed for causing the darkness.

Several eclipses have had a fateful effect in history, as recorded by the historians of Antiquity. Herodotus, in the fifth century B.C., recorded that when night fell in the middle of the day, the Medes and Lydians, who were fighting each other, were so frightened they made peace. Theucydides (fifth century B.C.) and Livy (first century B.C.) noted that an eclipse occurred before two major battles, those of Syracuse and Pydna.

The *Tetrabiblos* by Ptolemy (second century A.D.) produced a scientific explanation, yet beliefs persisted and influenced the morale of the armies. In 1453, an eclipse of the moon precipitated the fall of Constantinople. In 1917, Lawrence of Arabia captured the Fort of Aqaba, in the Sinai desert, in similar circumstances.

The two great discoverers, Alexander the Great and Christopher Columbus, both knew how to take advantage of the fear inspired by this cosmic paradox. Traditionally, in fact, the only people threatened are kings and heads of state. A total eclipse of the sun occurred, for example, on July 20, 1963, and John Fitzgerald Kennedy was assassinated on November 23 of the same year.

From an astronomical point of view, an eclipse is the result of temporary obscuration by a passing heavenly body. The phenomenon occurs when the moon reaches the ecliptic, and is thus close to its Nodes. In an eclipse of the sun, the (new) moon passes between the sun and the Earth; depending on the height of the moon in its orbit, the eclipse may appear total, partial, or annular. In an eclipse of the moon, the (full) moon enters the cone of the Earth's shadow. An eclipse of the sun is always preceded or followed by an eclipse of the moon. These phenomena are produced with a foreseeable regularity, depending on the cycle of Saros. In a given location, eclipses of the moon appear much more frequently than those of the sun, on average every two years for the former, as opposed to every few decades for the latter.

In an individual horoscope, the eclipse reveals the imperfections of a situation, symbolized by the House in question, and makes it possible to correct them; the effect lasts for about six months until the next eclipse.

Views of a total eclipse of the sun on August 30, 1905. Algiers Observatory.

FIXED STARS

CELESTIAL PUNCTUATION

"I see stars, and stars, and stars;
I see constellations, and constellations, and constellations;
I see mixed rays with knotted splendors
In flames and lost flashes of light
in contemplations, contemplations plunged
into flashes of light; I am caught up in a prodigious
turning of the wheel with a golden nave.
Where is it going? I know nothing of it.
The night is the beaten track of the stars."

VICTOR HUGO, On Jersey (1854, trans.)

STARS TWINKLE LIGHT YEARS AWAY FROM THE EARTH, FAR OUTSIDE THE SOLAR SYSTEM, YET SOME OF THEM MOVE SO SLOWLY ACROSS THE arc of the zodiac that they give the impression of being immobile. Hipparchus, who lived in the second century B.C., was the first to make an inventory of the stars. Three centuries later, Ptolemy dubbed them *fixed stars*, an appellation which has remained ever since. From 1789 through 1798, the French astronomer Lalande noted the positions of fifty thousand stars in his *Histoire céleste française*. Astrology currently takes account of about a hundred fixed stars, being those which are in conjunction of up to two *degrees of orb* with the planet of a chart.

THE FIXED STARS IN THE SIGNS
(Positions calculated for the year 2000)

In Aries: *Alpherat*, at 14°08', provides humanitarian interests and love of animals. On the other hand, *Alderamin*, at 12°49', and Algenib, at 8°09', are inauspicious.

In Taurus: *Mirach*, at 0°24', brings charm and goodness. *Triangle*, at 6°49, offers beauty. *Chedir*, at 7°48', and *The Pleiades*, at 29°49', confer artis-

tic gifts. On the other hand, *Algol*, at 26°07', is negative and violent.

In Gemini: *Aldebaran*, at 09°44', confers popularity. *Rigel*, at 16°49', inspires renown. *Betelgeuse*, at 28°44', indicates riches.

In Cancer: *Sirius*, at 14°04', inspires pride and passion. *Castor*, at 20°14', promises intelligence and literary success. *Pollux*, at 23°14' means fear with a risk of accident.

In Leo: *Regulus*, at 29°44', brings ambition and generosity.

In Virgo: *Denebola*, at 21°37', evokes nobility, *Copula*, at 25°11', erotic passion, *Zavijava*, at 27°06', force of character and *Markeb*, at 29°16', good luck through travel.

In Libra: *Spica* (wheat ear), at 23°44', promises talent and renown. *Arcturus*, at 24°14', inspires wealth and honors.

In Scorpio: *Accrux*, at 11°49', which shines in the *Southern Cross*, inspires a taste for mystery and a sense of ceremonial. *Agena*, at 23°49', promises honors. As for *Bungala*, at 29°34', it indicates a bent for the occult.

In Sagittarius: *Antares*, at 09°44', brings intelligence and energy.

In Capricorn: *Spiculum*, at 0°56', is an ill omen, because it symbolizes depression and eye troubles. *Vega*, at 15°19', is famous for bestowing musical gifts and the promise of riches.

In Aquarius: *Altair*, at 1°44', brings courage and elevation.

In Pisces: *Acharnar*, at 15°14', confers quite strong occult powers.

Measuring the Angles. German wood engraving, circa 1530.

OTHER ASTROLOGIES

OTHER HEAVENS

ASTROLOGY IS AN ART OF THE PEOPLE WHICH, LIKE GOOD WINE, BEARS THE IMPRINT OF ITS NATIVE SOIL AND CHANGES OVER time. Each civilization has its own form of astrology, one that is a reflection of its own culture and history. The symbols and rules of interpretation, the heritage of a very ancient tradition, are constantly being updated in light of scientific progress, philosophical theories, travel, and changes of lifestyle. Chinese, Indian, and Arab cosmogonies are very different from our own but draw their inspiration from traditions thousands of years old. However, mythologies are now merging even more quickly than in Marco Polo's day. The Chinese bestiary has become familiar to Westerners and the astrology of the constellations, an Indian influence, is gradually gaining ground. In the Age of Aquarius and the Internet, a cosmopolitan form of astrology derived from a mixture of origins is required— from which individuals can draw the teaching which suits them.

CHINESE ASTROLOGY

"He who does not know his nature will never achieve his destiny."

CONFUCIUS (circa 555–479 B.C.)

In China, *divination* holds an extremely important place in social life. It influences existence and plays a part in each significant event, from birth to burial—career, marriage, travel, and health. In addition to the horoscope, it takes three official forms: the imperial almanac, the *Yi-King*, and *Feng-Shui*.

Unlike in the West, the accent is never on the individual, his potential and accomplishments, but on the collective, the family, the village, or town, in which the individual lives. As in an orchestra, each instrument plays its part but it is the general harmony which is important. This accord rests on the balance of forces present, the *Yin* (sentimental, feminine, and passive) and the *Yang* (energetic, masculine, and active.)

The Chinese do not believe in the influence of the planets on destiny. The planets are only used to measure time because, according to Confucius, down here "everything flows by." At birth, the horoscope establishes *the four pillars of destiny*: one for the year, one for the month, one for the day, and one for the hour. Contrary to Western practice, where considerations of the sign and Ascendant are freely given, the Chinese prefer to keep the pillars of the month, day and time secret: "One only emerges from one's ambiguity to one's own detriment," states a popular proverb. Soothsayers and doctors are clearly bound by professional secrecy.

The Chinese astrological year is based on solstices and equinoxes, culminating moments in the season. The moon phases and its twenty-seven abodes punctuate the year. Chinese astrology is lunar and divinatory. The study of the birth chart involves evoking the qualities and powers of the four pillars and their relationship to each other. Furthermore, an *agent* is associated with each pillar: wood, fire, earth, metal, or water, each defining a particular type of energy.

Pandit Anand Shankar Vyas, a famous Indian astrologer.

The cycle of Jupiter is used as the starting point: it lasts for twelve years and is called the *Great Year*. It inspired the division into twelve legendary beasts—those who answered Buddha's call and who appeared in the following order.

The Rat: 1900, 1912, 1924, 1936, 1948, 1960, 1972, 1984, 1996, 2008.

Rats are opinionated, meticulous, sociable, energetic, and sentimental. However, they are accused of being restless, suspicious, and miserly.

The Buffalo: 1901, 1913, 1925, 1937, 1949, 1961, 1973, 1985, 1997, 2009.

The Buffalo is supposed to be methodical, organized, precise, balanced, economical and hardy. He is sometimes accused of being naturally slow and conventional, jealous, and rancorous.

The Tiger: 1902, 1914, 1926, 1938, 1950, 1962, 1974, 1986, 1998, 2010.

Tigers are described as generous and strong, powerful, magnetic, authoritarian, personal, but also disciplined, proud, inflexible, and rash.

The Hare: 1903, 1915, 1927, 1939, 1951, 1963, 1975, 1987, 1999, 2011.

Hares are supposed to be elegant and sociable, discreet and likeable, sensitive, subtle, ambitious, and affable, but hypocritical and distant, secretive, complex, and egotistical.

The Dragon: 1904, 1916, 1928, 1940, 1952, 1964, 1976, 1988, 2000, 2012.

Dragons are said to have panache, good at presenting themselves, magnetic, intuitive, artistically and socially influential, but they are also considered to be ostentatious, unrealistic, anguished, and dissatisfied.

The Serpent: 1905, 1917, 1929, 1941, 1953, 1965, 1977, 1989, 2001, 2013.

Serpents have a detached, reflective, calm, intuitive, and accommodating mentality, but if crossed, they may reveal themselves to be jealous, possessive, arrogant, cynical—in a word, poisonous.

The Horse: 1906, 1918, 1930, 1942, 1954, 1966, 1978, 1990, 2002, 2014.

This character is brilliant, eloquent, sociable, lively, intelligent, hard-working, conscious of his own limitations, but easy to anger, violent, sarcastic, and too sensitive to other people's opinions about him.

The Goat: 1907, 1919, 1931, 1943, 1955, 1967, 1979, 1991, 2003, 2015.

The Goat has an unruly but ambitious, rigorous temperament. He is refined, forward-looking, wise, and disciplined, but is also hair-splitting, critical, utopian, and dependent.

The Monkey: 1908, 1920, 1932, 1944, 1956, 1968, 1980, 1992, 2004, 2016.

The character of the Monkey is very much like the zoological descriptions of the animal. He is said to be quick-witted, inventive, intelligent, adroit, and active, but also opportunist, hypocritical, imitative, and dishonest.

The Rooster: 1909, 1921, 1933, 1945, 1957, 1969, 1981, 1993, 2005, 2017.

The Rooster is the symbol of candor, courage, elegance, enthusiasm, humor, and assurance, which may degenerate into ostentation, boastfulness, insolence, and eccentricity.

The Dog: 1910, 1922, 1934, 1946, 1958, 1970, 1982, 1994, 2006, 2018.

The Dog also has all the qualities its animal counterpart possesses: courage, loyalty, faithfulness, modesty, generosity, docility, but also cowardice, aggression, pessimism, introversion, and conservatism.

The Boar: 1911, 1923, 1935, 1947, 1959, 1971, 1983, 1995, 2007, 2019.

The Boar is a gullible hedonist, loyal and hardworking, enclosed within his professional conscience. Honest, scrupulous, placid, and accommodating, he is nevertheless subject to whims and incomprehensible fits of stubbornness.

Signs of the Chinese zodiac. 1915.

INDIAN ASTROLOGY

*"After death, the soul needs to release itself
From all its faults before inhabiting a new body,
Suited to its moral nature."*

PYTHAGORAS (6th century B.C.)

The first Indian astrological tables date from the most ancient times, before the Aryan invasions. In about 1800 B.C., the relationship between India and Mesopotamia favored a great leap forward in knowledge of the cosmos. Hindu writings, including the *Arthava Veda* (1500 B.C.), then the *Mahabharata* (500 B.C.), evoke the *twenty-seven abodes of the moon,* which are called *Nakchatras.*

The moon was and still is the primary indicator of time for the Indians. The Ancients divided the ecliptic into twenty-seven sections, thus giving rise to a lunar zodiac.

The twelve Chaldean signs were imported in about 325 B.C., at the time of the conquests of Alexander the Great. Later, there were productive exchanges with Arab astrology. The first ephemeris was printed in the late fifteenth century, as in the West. It should be noted that until the mid-twentieth century, British influence was very marked on the horoscope. Due to accidents of history, Indian astrology thus became the crucible in which various doctrines and techniques were fused.

The Indians continue to use the *starred sidereal zodiac.* The variation from the *tropical zodiac* is about eighty degrees, which have to be reworked to match the coordinates of the Western ephemeris. In practice, the operation results in moving backwards by an average of one sign; a Western Aries becomes a Pisces in India, and so on.

Interpretation is based on traditional combinations of planets, signs, Houses, and aspects.

Indian cosmogony grants a place of overwhelming importance to *Chandra,* the moon. Chandra represents a masculine entity, conquering and warlike, associated with the white of seminal fluid, and *Surya,* the sun, is a feminine entity linked to the scarlet of blood and the flamboyance of gold. There are five planets in the map of the Heavens: *Buddha* (Mercury), *Sukra* (Venus), *Mangala* (Mars), *Brihaspati* (Jupiter), and *Sani* (Saturn.) The twenty-seven abodes of the moon, to which special powers are attributed, constitute the foundation of the liturgical calendar. To this should be added *South and North Lunar Nodes, Ketu* and *Rahu* respectively, on which the doctrine of *karma* is based. For an Indian, the objective of his incarnation consists in accepting his karma, the consequences of his previous lives, and to assume his *dharma,* or higher mission.

Predictions are based on planetary periods, each age of life being governed by a particular body, in the order of the lunar abodes. The *retrograde planets* are considered to be ill omens. Finally, the Indians use the square to represent the birth chart. As the symbol of materialization, it is in opposition to the circle, the figure of eternity. Like the temples and mandalas, the square is a sacred character in India.

The Indian signs

(Deduct 23°50' from Western planetary coordinates.)

Aries: **Mesha**	Libra: **Thula**
Taurus: **Vrishaba**	Scorpio: **Vrishika**
Gemini: **Mithuna**	Sagittarius: **Dhanus**
Cancer: **Kataka**	Capricorn: **Makara**
Leo: **Simba**	Aquarius: **Kumba**
Virgo: **Kanya**	Pisces: **Meena**

*Preceding pages : astronomer observing the heavens with the help of an astrolabe.
Indian miniature, early 17th century.
Facing: the infinite serpent. Indian miniature, late 18th century.*

ولادت كثير السعادة شاهنشاه فلك بارگاه اسكندر جاه عرش كوكبه

آسمان دركاه خلايق اميد كاه سليمان جاه انجم سپاه عالم پناه ظل اله السلطان

ابن السلطان والخاقان ابن الخاقان ابن الخاقان المؤيد بتأييدات الملك

العزيز الغفار لازالت مدة ودولته طالعة من مطالع السعادة والاقبال و مانفكت

شموش شوكته ساطعة من مشارق الدولة والاجلال دريوم جمعه ششم شهر جمادى الاول

من شهور سنه شش شاعت و نحو دقيقه از طلوع آفتاب گذشته وقوع يافته است

ARAB ASTROLOGY

Arab astrology was born long before Mohammed, through the observation of the sky by tribes of nomads and caravans. Since caravans of camels traveled at night, the moon served as a light-giver and Venus as a guide. *Qama*, the masculine word for moon, thus became king of the pantheon, and *Shams*, the feminine word for the sun, became his wife. The cult of the heavenly bodies, linked to fetishism and magical rites, spread throughout the countries of the Mediterranean basin in the form of divination. From Antiquity to the Middle Ages, Indian and Greek thought influenced the Arabs, and made it possible to first create the *zairja*, or *ouija*, the circular table which was used to divine the Universe. The philosophical alphabet culminated in the foundation of logical calculus. Arab astrology also took material from the Kabbalah, geomancy, and divination by using sand. The protective genies or *djinns*, were gradually replaced by the names of weapons and armor. The measurement of time was a problem. Clepsydras (water-clocks) and sundials were the prerogative of the rich. In order to overcome the general ignorance as to the precise date and time of birth, an *hourly astrology* grew up, establishing the chart at the time when the consultant asked his question. In the eighth century, at the request of the Caliph Al-Mansur, the astrologer Messalhala calculated the date of the foundation of Baghdad (762). Ibn Ezra invented the system of domification, as well as the *thebaic calendar*.

The most famous Arab philosophers and mystics, such as Avicenna (980–1037) and Averroes (1126–98), believed in the astral influence over the terrestrial world but rejected fatalism completely. In fact, there is nothing in the Koran which proscribes astrology, and the heavenly bodies are thought to be indicators of divine will.

Even today, Arab astrologers always end by using a formula such as: "God alone holds the truth."

The choice of weapons
(see tables on following pages)

Several socio-cultural criteria are involved in the choice of Arab weapons and the numbers associated with them. The date of birth determines the *weapon of predestination*, equivalent to the traditional signs. *The weapon of ascendance* reflects family status. The third weapon, or *weapon of luck*, is linked to the place of birth: village, town, or city. The numeric combination of these weapons indicates the *weapon of birth*. Finally, the *weapon of arrival* represents the path and reflects the social position of the subject.

The arm of birth corresponds to the average of the three factors. When the numbers associated with each criterion are added up, the result is divided by three and rounded to the nearest whole number (*see third table, left-hand figure*).

Despite the weapons system, Arab astrologers also use traditional astrology. The following tables indicate the equivalents of Western signs and Arab weapons.

Facing page: horoscope of the Persian king, Qadjar Fath Ali Shah, Teheran, undated.
Following page: extract from the perpetual calendar (Ruznâmeh).
Ink, gouache and gold on paper, 1760.

The weapons of predestination

Date of birth	Sign	Weapon	Number
March 21–April 20	Aries	**Dagger**	2
April 21–May 21	Taurus	**Peasant club**	6
May 22–June 21	Gemini	**Iron bar**	5
June 22–July 22	Cancer	**Cutlass**	3
July 23–August 23	Leo	**Sword**	9
August 24–September 23	Virgo	**Knife**	1
September 24–October 23	Libra	**Chain**	8
October 24–November 22	Scorpio	**Arab dagger**	4
November 23–December 21	Sagittarius	**Bow**	12
December 22–January 20	Capricorn	**Lance**	10
January 21–February 18	Aquarius	**Slingshot**	11
February 19–March 20	Pisces	**Ax**	7

The weapon of ascendancy

Parents' occupation	Weapon
1. Underprivileged classes: unemployed, tramps, beggars	**Knife**
2. Servants: maids, workers, guards	**Dagger**
3. Craftsmen and merchants: sellers, valets, butlers, cooks, masons	**Cutlass**
4. Risky occupations: policemen, detectives, sportsmen, adventurers, prostitutes	**Arab dagger**
5. Leaders: officers, middle management, company secretaries, accountants	**Iron bar**
6. Occupations of the land: farmers, agronomists, gardeners	**Peasant club**
7. Intellectuals: teachers, technicians, publishers, journalists, actors	**Ax**
8. Industry, trade and the professions: senior management, bankers, insurers	**Chain**
9. Positions of power: ministers, senior officials, politicians, religious leaders	**Sword**
10. Leading intellectuals: professors, lawyers, surgeons, artists	**Lance**
11. Creative people: artists, composers, researchers, philosophers	**Slingshot**
12. Heros: exceptional people, internationally known	**Bow**

The weapon of chance

Place of birth	Weapon
1. Less than 500 inhabitants	**Knife**
2. From 500 to 2,000 inhabitants	**Dagger**
3. From 2,000 to 5,000 inhabitants	**Cutlass**
4. From 5,000 to 15,000 inhabitants	**Arab dagger**
5. From 15,000 to 30,000 inhabitants	**Iron bar**
6. From 30,000 to 100,000 inhabitants	**Peasant club**
7. From 100,000 to 200,000 inhabitants	**Ax**
8. From 200,000 to 350,000 inhabitants	**Chain**
9. From 350,000 to 600,000 inhabitants	**Sword**
10. From 600,000 to 1,500,000 inhabitants	**Lance**
11. From 1,500,000 to 5,000,000 inhabitants	**Slingshot**
12. More than 5,000,000 inhabitants	**Bow**

THE ABODES OF THE MOON

AN ORIENTAL APPROACH TO THE ZODIAC

ALL THE COSMOGONIES, WITH THE EXCEPTION OF WESTERN ASTROLOGY, REFER TO THE ABODES OF THE MOON. THIS IS A VERY ancient tradition which divides the course of the lunar orbit into abodes. There are as many abodes as there are days (27.8) in the lunar cycle, making twenty-seven *Nakchatras* in India (twenty-eight abodes for the Arabs and the Chinese.)

Indian astrology is probably the most accurate on this point. In an Indian chart, the lunar abode occupied by the sun is as important as the sign of the zodiac. These abodes have their own mythology, character, colors, and special features which create delightful portraits, for example: "liar and very musical" or "religious but rather uncharitable." Each abode is governed by a planet whose action combines with that of the sun sign. Thus, an Aries subject, ruled by Mars, could be co-governed by Venus, who reigns over the subject's birth Nakchatra.

From the astronomical point of view, the Nakchatras are counted from 0° Aries (tropic). Each covers 13°20', representing that portion of Heaven covered daily by the moon.

THE ABODES OF THE MOON AND THEIR MEANINGS IN INDIAN ASTROLOGY

(To use these, it is necessary to know the exact position of the sun. For example, if your sun is at 15° Taurus, its abode is Rohini, which is dominated by the moon, and you will be a Taurus, strongly influenced by the moon.)

Ashwini (00° – 13°20' Aries). Dominant: Ketu (South Lunar Node). Character: intelligent, cultivated, esteemed. Fairly wealthy.

Bharani (13°20' – 26°40' Aries). Dominant: Venus. Character: courageous, obliging, full of sex appeal. Few children.

Krittika (26°40' Aries – 10° Taurus). Dominant: Sun. Character: lucid, honest, greedy. Great riches.

Rohini (10° – 23°20' Taurus). Dominant: Moon. Character: cultivated, authoritarian, wealthy but ungrateful to mother.

Mrigasira (23°20' Taurus – 06°40' Gemini). Dominant: Mars. Character: active, corpulent, many dislikes.

Aridra (06°40' – 20° Gemini). Dominant: Rahu (North Lunar Node.) Character: pride, disloyalty, cunning, artful. Longevity.

Punarvasu (20° Gemini – 03°20' Cancer). Dominant: Jupiter. Character: good, likeable but weak, vulnerable.

Pushya (03°20' – 16°40' Cancer). Dominant: Saturn. Character: eloquent, intelligent, violent, crafty.

Ashlesha (16°40' – 30° Cancer). Dominant: Mercury. Character: courageous, authoritarian, tough. Unreliable. Children.

Magha (00° – 13°20' Leo). Dominant: Ketu (South Lunar Node). Character: work devotion, faith. Hatreds. Wealth and pleasures.

Purva Phalguni (13°20' – 26°40' Leo). Dominant: Venus. Character: generous, protective. Lack of courage.

Uttara Phalguni (26°40' Leo – 10° Virgo). Dominant: Sun. Character: beautiful, sensual, wealthy. Several marriages.

Hasta (10° – 23°20' Virgo). Dominant: Moon. Character: lascivious, cunning, intelligent. Travel.

Chitra (23°20' Virgo – 06°40' Libra). Dominant: Mars. Character: calculating and quarrelsome. Happiness in foreign lands. Loved by women.

Swati (06°40' – 20° Libra). Dominant: Rahu (North Lunar Node). Character: courteous, spiritual. No children. Not loved by own family. Travel.

Vishakha (20° Libra – 03°20' Scorpio). Dominant: Jupiter. Character: lucky in marriage and family. Wise.

Anuradha (03°20' – 16°40' Scorpio). Dominant: Saturn. Character: beautiful, mystical. Many travels.

Jyeshta (16°40' – 30° Scorpio). Dominant: Mercury. Character: spiritual, adaptable, irascible. Many children.

Moola (00° – 13°20' Sagittarius). Dominant: Ketu (South Lunar Node). Character: wealth, power, beauty. Dishonesty, versatility. Illness.

Purva Shadha (13°20' – 26°40' Sagittarius). Dominant: Venus. Character: faithful, humble, respectable. Conjugal stability.

Uttara Shadha (26°40' Sagittarius – 10° Capricorn). Dominant: Sun. Character: modest intelligent. Several unions. Travel.

Shravana (10° – 23°20' Capricorn). Dominant: Moon. Character: success, culture, wealth. Many dislikes. Good marriage, few children.

Dhanista (23°20' Capricorn – 06°40' Aquarius). Dominant: Mars. Character: talkative, musical, heroic, generous. Loves dancing.

Satabisha (06°40' – 20° Aquarius). Dominant: Rahu (North Lunar Node). Character: versatile, talkative, cunning, lucky. Few children.

Purva Bhadrapada (20° Aquarius – 03°20' Pisces). Dominant: Jupiter. Character: fortunate, sensual. Wealth and long life.

Uttara Bhadrapada (03°20' – 16°40' Pisces). Dominant: Saturn. Character: eloquent, timid, skillful, virtuous, wealthy.

Retavi (16°40' – 30° Pisces). Dominant: Mercury. Character: brave, proud, wealthy. Many dislikes. Longevity.

HOROSCOPES AND FORECASTS

THE ART OF PREDICTION

FOR A LONG TIME, ASTROLOGICAL PREDIC-TIONS WERE THE SOLE PRESERVE OF KINGS AND SOVEREIGNS WHO HELD THE DESTINIES of their country in their hands. The individual horoscope as we know it was first devised in Greece in the fifth century B.C. Today it is this form of astrology which has gained the lion's share in Western individualist cultures, relegating predictions of world events to second rank in the practice of astrology.

The personal horoscope is based on a study of the Heavens. The astrologer creates a psychological portrait of the subject, his options and plans in life as they appear from the celestial configurations. The astral theme can be read like a musical score with which the individual can do what he likes—or is capable of. The role of free will traditionally remains important in astrology. The state of the Heavens is obviously not the only factor. Each human being is subject to the laws of his or her environment, the dominant culture, social class and education—to say nothing of his or her karma. The interpretation of the chart is just one type of forecast. There are many other forms of prediction based on the observation of the planetary cycles.

The *solar revolution* is calculated at the time of the birthday. It is a map of the Heavens produced to show the date on which the sun will return to the position it had at the subject's birth, but in the current location. It contains within it the existential climate for the coming year. This forecasting technique, which became fashionable in the sixteenth century, is once again gaining ground in this age of frequent travel.

The *planetary transits* will cause one or more planets to intervene in the aspects they form at birth or in opposing aspects. The transit describes the passage of a planet at a sensitive point in the chart in such a way as to release dormant energies. A transit of a birth aspect is most effective when it is repeated.

Other techniques, such as *progressions* and *directions*, complete the types of forecasting possible on an individual basis.

World astrology only uses planetary transits. The Babylonians were much preoccupied by this very ancient form of horoscope which they invented. It merely deals with the fortunes of countries and kings, but requires some geopolitical knowledge and great familiarity with history. The map of the Heavens in the country in question is created to reflect a significant date—usually the date on which independence was proclaimed or a constitution introduced. Thus, post-war France's sign is Libra, as is that of the new Germany reunited in 1990 and the People's Republic of China declared in 1949. Switzerland is Virgo, Belgium Scorpio, the United Kingdom Capricorn, and the United States, born on July 4, Cancer. Russia happens to be Sagittarius, although the Soviet Union was Scorpio. Other

signs include India, under Leo, whereas Israel and Japan are Taurus. World astrology attaches great importance to eclipses of the sun and moon, as well as the passage of comets. This form of astrology is traditionally pessimistic, regularly heralding national or international disasters, universal catastrophes, floods, earthquakes, and apocalypses of every kind. It has proved to be quite relevant in political forecasting and in the past has supplied valuable indications of the resolution of diplomatic crises, border disputes, wars of succession, and so on.

A tradition dating back to the Middle Ages links astrology and *almanacs*. The *Shepherds' Calendar,* which began in the fifteenth century, was long used in the French countryside, and the *Vox Stellarum* and *Zadkiel Almanac,* and later *Old Moore's Almanac,* were similarly popular in England. The astrological almanac combined agricultural observations, gardening advice, and

portraits of the signs. In about 1930, the British introduced magazine horoscopes, which appeared mainly in the Sunday press and the national daily newspapers with their huge circulations. During World War II, almanacs became instruments of propaganda, based on astrological elements of varying degrees of reliability. After the war, magazine horoscopes took over, consigning most almanacs to history. Radio and television also made use of astrology, thus popularizing it even further.

The ultimate symbol of the 1980s, financial astrology, offered forecasts to the financiers of Wall Street, Paris, and London. The experts based their apparently carefully researched opinions on magnetic storms, sunspots, and eclipses of the moon. They claimed that astrology enabled them to predict geopolitical events and cyclical fluctuations which would influence the money markets and the economy.

Cover of an astrological almanac. 1859.

CONSULTATION

SACRED OR PAGAN RITE

CONSULTING AN ASTROLOGER INVOLVES A SPECIAL RITUAL WHICH PRESUPPOSES A CERTAIN MENTAL PREPARATION: STRESS MUST BE eliminated and the subject filled with positive energy, in a listening frame of mind. The ritual changes depending on whether the consultation takes place in New York, Paris, Hong Kong, or Cairo. It is a religious ritual in India, solemn in China, a magical rite in the East, pagan in the West. Whatever the latitude, a consultation represents a way of trying to find out about one's life, and put desires and possibilities into perspective, so as to find harmony with the cosmic energies.

INDIA

In India, time belongs to the gods and astrology is an integral part of the religion. The *Veda*, the name of the four books "revealed" by the divinities to the sages of the Vedic era, containing divine wisdom and probably the oldest known texts, are the foundation for Indian culture. They are recited at specific moments that are inscribed in the astrological calendar. Astrologers belong to the Brahmin caste and are consulted by all social classes. The astrologer's wisdom is transmitted from generation to generation and he refers constantly to the great masters, whose works he knows by heart. His role is somewhere between that of a physician and priest. He is responsible for removing the traps set by malevolent divinities, and to this end, he has recourse to the *mantras*, ritual prayers, and offerings. Astrology is used to determine the dates on which the major events of existence should be celebrated—births, marriages, and funerals, in order to place them under the best auspices. There is also recourse to an astrologer each time an important venture is planned, such as a trip, a major purchase or sale, a family reunion, or moving house.

THE ARAB COUNTRIES

In Arab countries, time-based astrology is generally used. The subject often does not know his or her precise date of birth which makes it impossible to calculate a chart of the Heavens. Instead, the astrologer casts the horoscope for the time when the question was asked. The consultation takes the form of an analysis of the omens linked to the position of the moon. Whatever the result of the divinations, God is thanked. Frequently, the astrologer is asked to devise protective talismans, designed for the whole family. Astrologers are consulted on everyday matters, about commercial transactions and love life, or about the health of a relative or friend. Astrologers often use other forms of divination, such as geomancy—reading the future in the sand—and divination by casting bones or shells, as well as rituals which may involve white magic.

CHINA

In China, astrology is associated with two other forms of divination, *Yi-King* and *Feng-Shui*. There is also the division into *Yin* or *Yang*, the

*The Astrologer. Engraving by Nicolas de Larmessin,
from the series "Customs of the trades and professions." Circa 1695, colored at a later date.*

eight hexagrams, nine colors, and twelve animals of Buddha. All these make up a complex symbolism that enables the astrologer to codify acts of daily life. The publication of the annual calendar is the occasion for special ceremonies at the time of the solstices. The Chinese also remain fond of lunar calendars. For over a century, the family of the venerable Mr. Choi has published an almanac in Hong Kong which sells nearly a million copies. It gives the most favorable days for the pursuit of certain rituals—marriage, birth, burial, and the most auspicious times for each sign.

Astrologers sit in little booths opening on the street where they see their private clients. They are consulted before each important decision is made. It is by no means unusual for pregnant women to give birth by cesarian section in order to ensure that the birth date of their child coincides with the most favorable predictions of the astrologer. Industrialists and traders will choose the date for opening their stores and starting their corporations on the basis of the position of the planets and the conclusions of Chinese geomancy. The *Tao* ("The Way"), the principle of wisdom, inspires an attitude of spiritual respect and practical confidence in these ancient methods of divination, which are combined with Chinese astrological prediction.

THE UNITED STATES AND EUROPE

In the United States and Europe, the introduction of the computer and software has made it much easier to cast a horoscope. A subject generally knows his date of birth to the nearest fifteen minutes. A wide range of people, drawn from all levels of society, consults astrologers. Planetary symbolism seems to be particularly important in urban settings where the seasons have little effect. Astrologers are consulted about romance, marital problems, questions of work and money—and occasionally, more rarely, about health.

The astrologer differs from the fortuneteller in that he or she avoids making predictions as to events, which are too uncertain, and tries instead to portray them as difficulties to be resolved as part of spiritual growth. It is on a symbolic level that individual potential and important dates are interpreted as part of the birth chart. However, when a worried client is in need of reassurance or requires a prompt reply, the astrologer often plays the role of an advisor. In the United States, an astrological consultation is often accompanied by a tarot reading and numerology session. In some cases, the astrologer may also be a medium, which makes his or her opinion all the more valuable. Astrologers, like fortunetellers and psychoanalysts, may be in or out of fashion. A good interpretation always tries to compromise between predestination and free will. "The stars incline, but never determine," wrote Ptolemy, eighteen centuries ago. Even in the computer age, there is nothing to contradict him.

STARS AND THE HUMAN BODY

THE ZODIACAL MAN

"A good physician needs to know astrology."

HIPPOCRATES (circa 460–377 B.C.)

THE CUSTOM OF CASTING A HOROSCOPE AS PART OF A PATIENT'S TREATMENT DATES BACK TO THE MOST ANCIENT TIMES. IN THE famous *Corpus Hippocratum*, Hippocrates, the father of medicine wrote, "Astrology is not trivial but of prime importance in the art of medicine." Around 332 B.C., Alexander the Great founded the school of medicine in Alexandria to which learned men flocked from all over the Mediterranean. The most famous of them, Galen, born in Pergamon (circa 131–201 A.D.), would dominate medicine for nearly a thousand years. Ptolemy (circa 90–168 A.D.), who was considered an expert in astrology, also taught in Alexandria. In his *De Metodo Metendi*, Galen reports some of this teaching: "The state of the heavens, the season of the year, the region, and the country must be taken into consideration in making the diagnosis and treating the illness." Inspired by Assyrian, Egyptian, and Babylonian observations, Galen later published a work entitled *How to Diagnose Illnesses Through Astrology*.

The practice was adopted by Imperial Rome. The *Astronomicon de Manilius*, written during the reign of Augustus, introduces the concept of zodiacal man, in which each organ of the body is governed by a sign of the zodiac. When the Roman Empire disintegrated, this knowledge fell into disuse. It was revived several centuries later among the Arabs through the influence of Jewish scholars at the School of Alexandria. In the eighth and ninth centuries, the Jews were considered to be the masters of astrology. As heirs of the tradition, they imbued it with their own forms of mysticism.

Astrology re-emerged in Europe in the Middle Ages, where it was taught at the universities of Toledo and Cordoba in Spain. Astrological medicine constituted an important part of the teaching. Kings, popes, and lords joined the scholars and became skilled in the art. In the sixteenth century, Charles V of France studied astrology under Adrian Floriszoon, the future pope Adrian VI. Catherine de Medici employed the services of Michel de Notre-Dame (Nostradamus) (1503–66), an astrologer-physician who owed his reputation to his care of victims of the Plague in 1546. Nostradamus was a Jew who had converted to Christianity. He practiced diagnosis based on the planetary aspects, prepared and used remedies made from plant extracts according to their astral correspondence, believed in critical days for certain patients, and used several basic rules of hygiene.

Astrological medicine was completely abandoned in the eighteenth century and fell into disuse with the advent of a totally scientific approach, at least in the West. Other cultures

Medieval map of the influence of the stars on the human body.

† τὸ μὲν ἥλιος διέρχεται τὰ ιβ' ζώδια ἐν τῷ ἐνιαυτῷ, εἰς διακοσίας ἑξήκοντα καὶ ... ἡμέρας· ποιῶν εἰς ἕκαστον ζώδιον μῆνα ἕνα. ἡ δὲ σελήνη διέρχεται τὸν ... κύκλον, εἰς ἡμέρας κη' ... ποιοῦν εἰς ἕκαστον ζώδιον, ἡμέρας β' ς'.

† νοητέον ὅτι ... ἡ σελήνη, εὑρίσκεται μετὰ τοῦ ... ζώδιον ... ἡμέρας ... διέρχεται τὰ ... ζώδια, εἰς ἡμέρας κη' ς'. ὅταν ... ἡ σελήνη ... ζώδιον,
προσέχειν ἵνα μὴ ποιῇ τομὴν ... εἰς τὸ μέλος ἐκεῖνο ὅπερ ἄρχει τὸ ζώδιον.

an. 32 usq. ad an. 48.

en 1556, sur le bruit de ses prophéties, henry 2 et Catherine de Médicis
firent venir à la Cour le médecin astrologue Michel Nostradamus, pour le
consulter sur le sort de leurs sept enfants; cet adroit personnage se tira
merveilleusement bien d'une position aussi difficile, et reçut 200 écus d'or.

continued to give it priority. In the Hindu religion, for example, a human has three separate bodies—the astral body, linked to the planets, the mental body, which governs thought, and the physical body, the seat of animal instinct. One cannot be treated without the other. The diagnosis must take into account the astral affinities and propitious periods for treatment.

Under the influence of mild medication and oriental practices at the turn of this century, astrology is timidly making a comeback in Western medicine. Although it is no longer as important as before, it is nevertheless a good psychological and physiological adjunct to diagnosis. A number of homeopaths, and even allopaths, consult the horoscope in order to be certain of the terrain before attacking the illness itself. In France, government-sponsored researchers are trying to establish a link between the astrological meridians and those used by acupuncture. East and West are united, as is man in the cosmos. A great start to the Age of Aquarius.

THE HUMAN BODY AND THE SIGNS OF THE ZODIAC

Each of the twelve signs governs a part of the body.

Sign	Part of the body
Aries	Head, brain, pituitary gland.
Taurus	Throat, face, thyroid.
Gemini	Chest cavity, bronchiae, arms and hands, thymus.
Cancer	Chest, stomach, lungs.
Leo	Spinal cord, spine, heart, liver, pancreas.
Virgo	Intestines, digestive secretions, stomach.
Libra	Kidneys, lumbar vertebrae, renal glands, hips.
Scorpio	Bladder, genitals, anus and large intestine.
Sagittarius	Pelvis, hips, thighs, femur.
Capricorn	Legs and knees.
Aquarius	Ankles and legs.
Pisces	Feet and immune system.

Henri II and Catherine de Medicis asking Nostradamus about the fate of their seven children. Print, 1558.

GLOSSARY

AFFLICTION: This ancient term designates a planet that is ill-disposed in relation to one or more others. The affliction results from its position in the zodiac (for example: *falling* in a sign) and the evil aspects it receives.

AGENT: Term used in Chinese astrology to indicate the five elements, wood, fire, metal, earth, and water.

ALBUMASAR: Albumasar was dubbed the Prince of Astrologers. He lived in Baghdad and died in 886. Albumasar adapted Ptolemy's *Catalogue of Fixed Stars*, giving the stars Arab names which they have retained. His book, *The Flowers of Astrology*, was one of the first to be printed by Gutenberg.

ANIMA MUNDI (SOUL OF THE WORLD): This is a Platonic term used to indicate the spiritual essence conferred by God in the celestial sphere at the moment of its creation. It consists of three categories: Existence, Identity, and Difference.

ASCENDANT: This astrological term designates the first House, centered at the eastern point of the horizon, where the zodiac rises.

ASTEROID: Lump of rock circulating through the solar system. There are about 40,000 asteroids, the first of which, Ceres, was discovered by Piazzi in 1800.

ASTROLOGY: Word designating the study of the relationship between the geocentric Heavens and events on Earth.

ASTRONOMY: Science of the relative positions of the movements, structure and changes in the heavenly bodies.

CARDINAL POINTS: From the apparent path of the sun, the Ancients deduced the symbolism of the cardinal points. The east, when the sun rises, is a country of light, life, and rebirth. The west, in which it sets, is the region of shadows. In India, however, the land of the dead lies in the south.

CELESTIAL MERIDIAN: Line of the celestial sphere which connects the North Pole and South Pole, passing above a point on the Earth.

CHIRON: Asteroid discovered in 1977 by the astronomer Charles Kowal, on the basis of a theory produced by the American astrologer Dane Rudhyar. Chiron occupies an orbital niche situated between Saturn and Uranus; it takes about fifty years to complete its orbit. In mythology, Chiron is associated with the legend of the Centaurs. Its symbolism refers to the idea of curing and the path to initiation.

CONJUNCTION: An aspect of 0° through 10° between two or more planets occupying the same sign. It reinforces the influence of the planets and the sign.

CONSTELLATIONS (OF THE ZODIAC): Visible groups of stars through which the ecliptic moves. Astrology counts twelve of them, the names of which have been given to the signs of the zodiac.

COPERNICUS: Polish astronomer (1473–1543) who shook the world by overturning Ptolemy's geocentric system which dated from the second century A.D. He never renounced his belief in the planetary influences. His master work, *De Revolutionibus Orbium Caelestium*, published in 1543, was an explanation of his new system of cosmogony: heliocentrism.

COSMOGONY: Mythological stories of the creation of the cosmos and formation of the heavenly bodies.

COSMOLOGY: Unlike cosmogony, cosmology is the science of the structure, origin and evolution of the Universe.

CULMINATION: This astronomical term designates the highest point in Heaven attainable by a heavenly body, at the intersection of its circle of declension with the meridian.

CUSPID: This designates the point of an astrological House.

DECAN: Division of a sign of the zodiac into three 10° segments.

DECLENSION: This is the measurement of the angle formed between the direction of the equatorial plane and the direction of the star, as seen by a notional observer standing at the centre of the Earth. It is said to be positive if it extends northward of the Earth, negative if it is descending southward.

DESCENDANT: This astrological term designates the seventh House, corresponding to the western point on the horizon at which the sun sets.

DOMINANT: Term designating a very strong planet in the astral chart. The dominant is found by applying various criteria which vary according to the schools of astrology.

ECLIPTIC: Apparent path of the sun around the Earth, passing through various constellations of the zodiac.

FALL: This term indicates the position of a planet in the zodiac where it has minimal influence. For example, Venus is *in fall* in the sign of Virgo.

GREGORIAN CALENDAR: This calendar was produced at the request of Pope Gregory XIII (1502–85), and introduced on October 4, 1582. It was designed to correct the differential of the tropical Julian calendar. It deleted ten days and created bissextile or leap years.

EXALTATION : This ancient term designates the position of a planet in the zodiac in which it exercises its maximum influence. For example, Venus in Pisces is in *exaltation*.

FENG-SHUI : Literally, "wind and rain." This is the term for an ancient form of Chinese divination or geomancy that obeys ancestral rules. *Feng-Shui* determines which places are beneficial and opportune for each person in a country, town, and home based on magnetic fields and other influences established at birth.

GANESH: The Hindu elephant-god, protector of astrologers.

GEOCENTRISM: Name of the system which places the Earth at the center of the Universe. It is applied particularly to the system invented by Ptolemy (second century A.D.), which dominated astrology until the time of Copernicus (1473–1543) and the discovery of the solar system.

HELIOCENTRISM: Name of the system devised by Copernicus which places the sun at the center of the universe.

HIPPARCHUS: Greek astronomer and mathematician (second century B.C.), who produced the first true catalogue of stars and discovered the precession of the equinoxes. He is also the inventor of the diopter and the astrolabe, both astronomical scientific instruments.

KEPLER : German astronomer and astrologer (1571–1630), who reinforced the foundations of astronomy and revived astrology. His laws concerning the movement of the planets are still used today. In his *Harmonia Mundi,* he reconciled science and mysticism.

LATITUDE : Angular distance of a point on the surface of the Earth from the equator. It is positive toward the north and negative toward the south.

LONGITUDE : Angular distance from a point on the Earth's surface at the Greenwich meridian, eastward or westward, which is converted into time based on the various time zones.

LUMINARIES: Ancient term designating the sun and moon.

LUNAR NODES: Points of intersection of the lunar orbit and the ecliptic. In Indian astrology, the two lunar nodes are the key to previous lives. The South Lunar Node (*Ketu*) symbolizes karma. The North Lunar Node (*Rahu*) is the objective of current incarnation.

MAGNITUDE : Apparent brightness of a star when seen from Earth. Depending on the degree of brilliance, Hipparchus (second century B.C.) classified the Heavens into six groups of magnitude (later refined by modern astronomy.) The stars of the first magnitude are Regulus, Antares, Spica, Pollux, and Aldebaran.

MANDALA : A religious drawing used by Indian and Tibetan Buddhists for meditation and drawing a map of their temples.

NATIVITY: Ancient term designating the horoscope at birth.

NOSTRADAMUS : French physician and astrologer (1503–66), descendent of the tribe of Issachar, Jacob's fifth son, who, according to tradition, possessed the power of divination. Persecuted as a Jew by the Inquisition, he led a nomadic life, but helped to rid the town of Aix of an epidemic of the Plague. He settled at Salon in southern France in 1547, where he created a laboratory and an observatory. His *Centuries* (1555), sibylline predictions written in alexandrine verse, are still avidly consulted.

OPPOSITION : The aspect of an 180° angle between two planets, considered to be dynamic.

ORB: The orb represents a tolerance in degrees plus or minus the angular value of an aspect. For example, the trine is an aspect of 120°, whose accepted orb is 8°, making an angle of 112° through 128°.

POLE STAR: Important star in mythology belonging to the constellation of Ursa Minor that now revolves around the celestial North Pole.

PRECESSION OF THE EQUINOXES: Retrograde movements of the points of the equinox due to the fact that the Earth inclines on its axis. The phenomenon was discovered by Hipparchus circa 140 B.C. It moves about 30° every two thousand years.

PTOLEMY: Astronomer and Greek physician (90–168), who lived in Alexandria at the time of Roman domination, and wrote the *Tetrabiblos*. His cosmographic system based on geocentrism was predominant in Europe until the eighteenth century.

RETROGRADE: The planets move at different speeds, Mercury and Venus moving faster than Earth, the others more slowly. At certain moments, from the terrestrial point of view, a planet appears to be moving backward. Traditionally, this movement is symbolized by the letter R. It tends to diminish the attributes of the planet and emphasize its defects.

RIGHT-HAND ASCENSION: This astronomical expression indicates the time, measured in hours, minutes and seconds, between the moment when the first point of Aries crosses the meridian and the moment when the celestial body crosses the same point on the meridian. The right ascension and declension constitute the coordinates of a planet or star.

SEXTILE: The aspect of a 60° angle between two planets, considered to be favorable.

SIDEREAL YEAR: Period of time needed by the sun to occupy the same point in relation to the stars (365,263 days). The difference from the tropical year is due to the *precession of the equinoxes*.

SQUARE: Angular aspect of 90° between two planets, considered to be dynamic.

THEBAIC CALENDAR: This calendar was devised in the Middle Ages by the astrologer Abraham Ibn Ezra. It associates each of the 360° of the zodiac with a symbolic image.

TRINE: Aspect at an angle of 120° between two planets, considered to be favorable.

TROPICAL YEAR: This is the period of time between two passages of the sun through the vernal point (365,242 days).

TYCHO BRAHE: Born forty-three years to the day after Nostradamus, this Danish astronomer (1546–1601) cast horoscopes for King Frederick II of Denmark, who built him an observatory. Brahe became the protégé of King Rudolph II of Bohemia. His observations on the movements of Mars enabled Kepler to reform astronomy.

YI-KING: In China, the *Yi-King*, or *Book of Changes*, is the foundation for wisdom and divination.

YOGA: In Indian astrology, the term designates a planetary association. There are hundreds of Yogas, each of which is defined in the manuals.

BIBLIOGRAPHY

BOSMAN, Leonard. *The Meaning and Philosophy of Numbers*. Rider & Co., 1974.

EBERTIN, Reinhold. *Astrological Healing: The History and Practice of Astromedicine*. Weiser, 1989.

GREENE, Liz. *Mythic Astrology*. Simon & Schuster, Inc., 1994.

GREENE, Liz and Howard Sasportas. *The Inner Planets: Building Blocks of Personal Reality*. Samuel Weiser, 1993.

JUNG, C.J. *Modern Man in Search of a Soul*. Harcourt Brace, 1955.

———. *Synchronicity: An Acausal Connecting Principle*. Princeton University Press, 1988.

LEWI, Grant. *Astrology for the Millions*. Llewellyn Publications, 1992.

———. *Heaven Knows What*. Llewellyn Publications, 1997.

MAYO, Jeff. *The Astrologer's Astronomical Handbook*. Fowler & Co., 1965.

PTOLEMY, *Ptolemy Tetrabiblos*, trans. F.E. Robbins. Harvard University Press, 1980.

SHARMAN-BURKE, Juliet and Liz Greene. *The Astrologer, the Counsellor, and the Priest*. CPA, 1997.

RENHART, Melanie. *Chiron and the Healing Journey: An Astrological and Pscyhological Perspective*. Penguin USA, 1989.

RUDHYAR, Dane. *The Astrology of Personality*. Aurora Press, 1991.

SCHERMER, Barbara. *Astrology Alive*. The Crossing Press, 1997.

SEYMOUR, Percy. *The Scientific Basis of Astrology*. St Martin's Press, 1992.

TOMPKINS, Sue. *Aspects in Astrology*. Element Books, 1991.

PHOTOGRAPHIC CREDITS

Spiritual homage is due to the masters no longer with us:
Joëlle de Gravelaine, Jean Carteret, Dane Rudhyar, Alexandre Ruperti.
The author would also like to thank Laurence Stasi,
of Editions Assouline, for her valuable artistic assistance
and to thank Pascal Barré, the information technology expert.

The publisher would like to thank Marie-Hélène Bayle,
of the Institut du Monde Arabe in Paris, the photographers Jean-Loup Charmet,
Jean-Paul Dumontier, Werner Forman, Roland
and Sabrina Michaud, Jean-Louis Nou, R. Perrin, and Jürgen Sorges,
as well as Bernard Garrett and Hervé Mouriacoux (AKG Paris),
the agencies Artephot, Ciel & Espace, Explorer, Galaxy Contact, Rapho,
Scala, and the French National Library
for their contributions to the production of this work.